DOES ANYONE CARE FOR HAITI?

Published by Jukejoint Publishing
P. O. Box 260835
Hartford, CT 06126-0835
e-mail address: jukejointb@aol.com

Deadly Road to Democracy
Copyright 1998
Marc Yves Regis I and Franki V. Regis
All rights reserved.

First Edition
First printing in the U.S. 1998

Library of Congress Cataloging-in-Publication Data

Cip-98-65802

ISBN 0-9663952-0-4

Photographs by Marc Yves Regis I

Book Design: Joseph Hilliman

Photo Editor: Cecilia Préstamo

Book Editor: Kent A. Miles

DEADLY ROAD TO DEMOCRACY

ACKNOWLEDGMENTS

Many people pitched in to help me complete this book. My deepest thanks goes to my dear friend Jocelyn Stewart, who is responsible for the final draft of this book. Without her keen insight, this book would not have been written. She traveled to Haiti with my wife and me during the summer of 1996. After reading the first manuscript, she wrote a critical analysis that helped me write a more personal story.

I'm grateful to Don Bohning for sharing with me his knowledge of Haiti, and offering invaluable factual advice.

Among the friends who read the manuscript and made suggestions on improving it, I would like to thank David Gibson, Courtney Anderson, Jean-Claude Bazelais, Dr. Carlo Jarda and his wife Marie-Jeanne Jarda, Andre Barnett and Karen Hunter. I also thank my colleagues at the Hartford Courant photography department, Shana Sureck-Mei, Stephanie Heisler, Thom McGuire and Dennis Yonan.

And, I thank my brother Andre Regis, who helped me with past and present events in Haiti. Without Andre, I would never have found a better life in the United States. In late 1980, he sent me all his savings — $1,000 — so I could leave Haiti after my life was in danger.

And finally, special thanks to my childhood friend in Haiti, Lesly Jean, who guided me in the right direction, and all my other friends who did not want their names used for safety reasons.

DEDICATION

I dedicate this book to the homeless children who live in the streets of Haiti and are rotting in misery.

May God bless them.

TABLE OF CONTENTS

FOREWORD

Marc Yves Regis I captures the essence of Haitian politics in his book "Deadly Road to Democracy." He chronicles Haiti's first experience in democracy through his eyes and the eyes of his mother. The book begins with the preparation for elections under the reign of Ertha Pascal-Trouillot, Haiti's first woman president. Marc Yves presents a powerful and insightful look into the behind-the-scenes maneuvers which have characterized Haitian politics since 1804. He eloquently chronicles the rise to power of Jean-Bertrand Aristide, with his many unfulfilled promises to the poor, and his demise at the hands of Lieutenant General Raoul Cedras during the coup that forced him into exile in 1991. Marc Yves graphically portrays the plight of the Haitian poor following imposition of the embargo on Haiti, and the irony of Aristide's return to Haiti on the backs of the same Americans he had so often criticized during his campaign and short-lived tenure as president. The irony was also not lost when Marc Yves pointed out that Aristide, the poor Roman Catholic priest, left the clergy to marry a member of the same bourgeois class he had chastised for not allowing the poor to eat at the same table and share in Haiti's wealth.

"Deadly Road to Democracy" is also about Marc Yves' personal tragedies and his search for meaning to the puzzling cycles of violence and vengeance that plague Haiti. He recounts the death of his brother in 1989 during a fight for freedom and justice, and going back to Haiti in 1992 in the midst of all the violence to bury his mother who had died. Marc Yves is not only a journalist reporting on the plight of Haitians, but he is an advocate on their behalf. Both Marc Yves and his wife, Franki, interviewed numerous people, including Ertha Pascal-Trouillot, for this book. They did it at great risk to their lives.

Marc Yves, who grew up poor like many of his fellow Haitians, conquered the obstacles that were in his way to become a successful photojournalist for Connecticut's largest newspaper. He attributes his success to the ideals imagined in him by his parents, particularly his mother. In this book, Marc Yves pays tribute to the resiliency of the Haitian people in their desperate struggle for justice. He empathizes with them in their never-ending war to overcome the chains of bondage that kept them from freely expressing their political views. Marc Yves has through this book written of another chapter in Haiti's history. It is by no means the last chapter.

Marc Yves has captured the essence of Haitian life through the lenses of his camera. His book presents a pictorial account of Haiti's past, present, and predictably the future. His photographs express the stark contrast between the excesses of the bourgeois and their multimillion-dollar mansions, and the desperation of the poor and their dilapidated huts. He shows cities ravaged by years of neglect, abuse and overpopulation. He also shows a countryside raped of all its natural resources and left barren to die in the hot tropical sun like a desert.

Most of all, Marc Yves' photographs are about the people of Haiti. You can feel the suffering from looking in the eyes of his subjects. You can experience their hunger for food and freedom. Their faces exhibit the scars of the repression and torture they have endured over the years. The young children in their freshly pressed uniforms, however, give some semblance of hope for a better future.

This book is a must read for anyone interested in the intricacies of Haitian politics and life. It is an outstanding literary and pictorial presentation.

Henri Alexandre
Connecticut Assistant State's Attorney

INTRODUCTION

So give us the bad news first . . .

At least four out of five people in Haiti cannot read. Three out of five don't get enough to eat. On average, people in this country cannot expect to live beyond 55 years. A quarter of Haiti's children won't make it to their fifth birthday. Tuberculosis leads a list of almost omnipresent diseases. The environment is disastrous; the forests of Haiti have been pillaged for firewood and charcoal. The middle class in this nation of 8 million people is tiny. Multinational investment is minuscule. Tourism is not far from dead. Jobs are scarce. Per capita, this is the country with the fewest telephones, the least electronic power, the lowest gross national product in the Western Hemisphere. There is no poorer, no unhealthier place to be found in this half of the world.

Ah, but there is hope.

From the people.

Each time I have visited Haiti these past several years, I have seen hope. The Haitians' own sense of optimism under frequently bleak conditions inspires me. I always depart this nation with the sense that if you could only help a few people here, and a few people over there, you could really make a difference because you are in the midst of so many people so willing to help themselves.

The manifestations of that optimism go far beyond putting up new structures, although there is a significant building "boom" as I write this. Far from significant for the people, who have suffered so much, Haiti has become a more "peaceful kingdom." A place of more safety and security. Haiti has found it does not need an army (under which so many abuses occurred over so many years), but it is training a police force whose mission is not to oppress the people, but to respect them and their rights. Human rights abuses have declined significantly. A system of justice and a judiciary are being built after lifetimes of neglect. Inflation has become more manageable. Young, progressive entrepreneurs have banded together to have a say in politics. Elections are being held, even if the turnout is puny. And more Haitians are staying home to build a nation.

But no one can deny — as Marc Yves Regis' words and pictures so poignantly and powerfully illustrate — that the journey remains painfully arduous.

Some history: It took a slave revolt against French colonialists for Haiti to become this hemisphere's second democracy, after our own. (Don't ever forget that Haiti dumped slavery six decades before we had the courage to do so in our own "land of the free and home of the brave.") To be sure, the years since 1804 have not resembled the kind of stable democracy Americans know. Over those 194 years, the Republic of Haiti had had 22 constitutions and 41 heads of state. (Nine of them declared themselves heads of state for life; 29 were assassinated or overthrown.) U.S. military rule marked the years from 1915 through 1934. In 1957, Dr. Francois Duvalier began a dictatorial reign whose brutality he would pass on to his son, Jean-Claude. An overthrow finally ended that tyranny in 1986. The next few

years meant nothing much better for Haiti. Optimism surfaced when Jean-Bertrand Aristide was elected president in 1990, but his overthrow the following year brought military rule once more. Three years later, the United States intervened, allowing for President Aristide's return. His successor would be Haiti's current elected president, Rene Preval.

A painful stretch of that history is covered in Marc Yves Regis' "Deadly Road to Democracy." He and I would not see Haiti exactly the same — we come from quite different experiences and cultures — but I have seen enough to know that this is a much-talented man who cares deeply and honestly about the land of his birth. This book focuses on the country's transition from dictatorship to democracy; even more, it focuses on the people of Haiti. You will see within these passages powerful photographic evidence of the violence and brutality, the despair — and the hope. Though he visits Haiti frequently, Marc Yves Regis leads us to discover that the Haiti one finds is always different from the country one has last departed. His work reflects a powerful procession of Haitian change that can be — sometimes all at once — devastating and inspiring.

The world knows little of Haiti's history. Nor has it cared much. Such ignorance and indifference should be humanity's shame. Outsiders know little beyond Haiti's French influence, of the voodoo culture that feeds so many stereotypes (80 percent of the country is Catholic), and of its grinding poverty. But there is so much more to know. So much more to give one hope.

I am fortunate to live in a part of the United States where my neighbors include a significant number of Haitians — more than 100,000 in South Florida. Many of them fled here from oppression. Others, like millions of other immigrants from other countries, came for economic gain. This book underscores the story of Haiti's unrelenting struggle for freedom. This book tells us how important "family" is to the Haitians. We witness that "family" in all the ways that Haitian Americans support their brothers and sisters in Haiti through hard work and the dollars they send home. These are people to admire.

Too often, the world has shrugged while Haiti has struggled in brutal and bloody circumstances. Humanity owes much more to Haiti.

Today we have come centuries past Haiti's earliest struggles for freedom. As the new century dawns, the struggles continue — in the streets of the capital of Port-au-Prince and in every rural village of Haiti; in Miami; in Washington; in the courts of the United States of America; in the United Nations. And Haiti endures. And Haiti hopes.

Marc Yves Regis tells this story so well. His great talents begin with a strong soul, a soul that embodies what I see so inspiring in the Haitian people.

From great suffering comes a special people. And a special book.

David Lawrence Jr.
Publisher, The Miami Herald

DEADLY ROAD TO DEMOCRACY

I

Women of Haiti,
queens of soul,
rhythms of spirits
who connect our blood,
our hearts, our souls
to our forefathers.
Get up and fight,
fight for liberation.

Women of Haiti,
queens of cheap labor
who are abused, exploited,
disrespected at the factories,
on the streets, at the markets.
Get up and fight,
fight for your rights.

Women of Haiti,
queens of courage,
who never abandoned their duties
as mothers, wives, sisters,
even at the price of their lives.
Get up and fight,
fight for your equality.

Women of Haiti
queens of dignity
it's time. . .
to rise above the humiliation
you bore for so, so long.
Women . . . of Haiti . . .
it's time.

7

MOTHER OF DEMOCRACY

My mother, Eulalu Desraline, grew up as most Haitians, with a muzzle on her mouth like a donkey saddled by repression. The muzzle passed from generation to generation, to my brother, three sisters, and me. We were not allowed to talk about freedom or democracy at home or in public. At home, my mother set the radio dial on the government-owned news station. Whenever any one of us tried to turn to an independent news station, my mother would say no, turn it back. She didn't want the government's secret police to beat her for listening to what they called propaganda.

We couldn't freely vote in elections; I never cast a vote in Haiti. When I fled my homeland for the United States in late 1980, I left my muzzle behind.

I had vowed to return one day and vote in my homeland when my country became politically stable. I had lived in Miami for six years when my country once again became embroiled in a political quagmire. In Miami, Haitian radio correspondents broadcasted from Haiti, describing how former President Jean-Claude "Baby Doc" Duvalier was ousted.

A succession of military governments held power from 1986 until 1990, when political protests and demonstrations organized by popular grass-roots groups in the country forced General Prosper Avril to resign after 18 months. Opposition leaders accused his military government of corruption and an unwillingness to hold national elections. He flew into exile to Florida aboard a U.S. Air Force jet. I knew he had failed to learn from his predecessors who had suffered the same fate. The U.S. government, which has a great deal of influence in Haiti, only supports strong leaders. When a ruler like Avril becomes weak, the United States is the first to give that leader a free ride out of Haiti and then choose another leader from its waiting list.

Supreme Court Justice Ertha Pascal-Trouillot was chosen in March 1990 as provisional president to replace Avril. My mother never heard about Pascal-Trouillot until she was appointed to head the interim government. Regardless, after 70 years of being tight-lipped about politics, my mother spoke in favor of Pascal-Trouillot.

My mother was delighted when a coalition of political, religious and civic leaders, desperate to end the bloodshed in Haiti, chose Pascal-Trouillot. Her job as provisional president was to govern and prepare the country for the first true democratic elections in Haiti since its nearly 200 years of independence from France.

I had never heard of Pascal-Trouillot while growing up in the slums of Port-au-Prince. It wasn't until 16 years after I left Haiti that I would meet her face to face. When I lived in Haiti, we were from different social classes. In Haiti, we have a saying that "the eagle flies with one wing." This wing represents 5 percent of the population that controls the country economically, socially and politically. The wealthy live in million-dollar houses, and drive expensive vehicles like Mercedes-Benzes and Jeep Cherokees. The missing wing represents the 95 percent of the population that possess nothing but misery. They are packed in one-room shacks surrounded by piles of trash.

Most Haitians knew about her late husband, Ernest Trouillot. He was a lawyer, teacher and journalist, and was popular in Haiti because of his involvement with the late Francois "Papa Doc" Duvalier, the former dictator of Haiti and the father of Baby Doc.

I was shocked when my mother told me, "Ertha is a good president."

"Why do you say that?" I asked.

"Because she cares," my mother answered.

I was baffled that my mother believed Pascal-Trouillot cared about the people, especially the poor. Why didn't my mother think Pascal-Trouillot was a crook, like the many Haitian leaders who had come before her? Besides, my mother never met the woman. They were from different backgrounds. My mother grew up poor and uneducated. Pascal-Trouillot was from a middle-class family and was well-educated.

But somehow, I understood my mother's blind support of Pascal-Trouillot. As a victim of Haiti's male-dominated society, my mother identified with the country's first woman president. Their economic and educational backgrounds were different, but psychologically, they were on the same level.

My mother felt it was a big accomplishment for the country that Pascal-Trouillot was named the first woman president in a male-chauvinistic society. In Haiti women give birth to life but they don't have a life. Throughout history, women have been exploited, abused, and disrespected. They have no rights. Their perceived roles include making babies, washing, cleaning and cooking.

Pascal-Trouillot's appointment was the first time I saw my mother's feminist side emerge. My mother, along with a lot of women, were happy; to them, Pascal-Trouillot represented all women. When she became president, women in Haiti seemed to forget that the Duvalier government appointed her as a judge. They overlooked that fact during their celebration for a woman president who somehow rubbed away the stigma of humiliation that women in Haiti faced for so long.

Nevertheless, I disagreed with my mother's blind support of Pascal-Trouillot. I joined ranks with my countrymen in Haiti and Miami's "Little Haiti" and protested against Pascal-Trouillot's appointment. It wasn't because she was a woman; it was because Duvalier appointed her to the Supreme Court and we didn't trust her. Most Haitians viewed her as a daughter of Duvalier. In Haiti, everything is based on loyalty, not merit. It was difficult for us to trust her or any judges in Haiti, where justice is sold like houses and cars. Judges are tainted by corruption. They falsify legal papers for friends who steal land from peasants. They use that land to build ranches and vacation homes. We know the faces of those who took land from peasants in the countryside and forced them to seek refuge in the ghettos of Port-au-Prince, on the shores of Miami and in the brutal sugar cane fields of the Dominican Republic.

Before Pascal-Trouillot took power, a series of coup d'états by military generals had pushed Haiti back down the road of hopelessness. Political leaders appointed Pascal-Trouillot and a 19-member civilian Council of State, a quasi-legislative group made up of representatives from various sectors of society. The council had veto power over the president's decisions. I later learned that several corrupt judges turned down the job. But that didn't prevent the middle-aged Pascal-Trouillot from trailblazing her way into the history books. At the time, she was the fourth woman to head a modern government in the Western Hemisphere. She was also the first woman to sit on the board of Port-au-Prince's bar association, the first woman appointed to a judgeship and the first woman on the Supreme Court.

Pascal-Trouillot's administration was the fourth to hold power since Baby Doc fled to France on Feb. 7, 1986, after months of tension and civil disorder. His departure ended 29 years of a brutal family dictatorship began by his father, Francois "Papa Doc" Duvalier, who declared himself president for life in 1964. Papa Doc maintained absolute political control while the country suffered from domestic political tension, corruption, severe repression and economic stagnation.

Pascal-Trouillot, however, had a difficult time flexing her political muscles during her 11 months of leadership. She clashed with the Council of State which demanded her resignation after she refused to consult with the advisory body. Council members accused her of acting like a dictator when she made independent decisions and allegedly allowed officials to raid the nation's coffers. The council severed all ties with the president and proposed an alternative government, which Pascal-Trouillot ignored. I finally realized what my mother knew all along — that women in Haiti, regardless of their social status, must fight for their rights in a male-dominated society.

The friction between the council and Pascal-Trouillot didn't surprise me because the council of 19 men felt humiliated for having to answer to a woman. It also reminded me of why the Duvaliers held power so long. Father and son ruled the country by clans. They knew that to be successful, they had to be united. Haitian leaders are typically selfish and power hungry. Only three months after Pascal-Trouillot took power, the council accused her of corruption and murder with help from the military. Ironically, while accusing Pascal-Trouillot of being a military puppet, members of the council were conducting back-door dealings with the same military. Some also had higher political aspirations and hidden agendas. The council wanted her to resign because she refused to collaborate with them. It's impossible to send a thief to catch a thief.

Still, Pascal-Trouillot was determined to complete her task of preparing the country for its first-ever democratic election. After she refused to resign, opposition groups made life miserable for her. Her social affairs minister, Claudette Werleigh, resigned from the 13-member cabinet. My mother said she understood that Werleigh may not have voted to endorse the

misappropriations of public funds and the dictatorship government, but where was Werleigh during the 29 years of Duvalier rule? Did she ever criticize the Duvaliers who emptied the country's coffers?

Werleigh's wavering is summed up in a Haitian proverb: "Dan pouri gen fos sou bannan mi." Rotten teeth are strong against ripe plantains.

The council blamed Pascal-Trouillot for killings of innocent people carried out by anti-democracy groups in broad daylight to create fear. One of the victims was Serge Villard, a member of the Council of State.

It was during this political turmoil that I visited Haiti to make sure my mother was all right. I was surprised to see Pascal-Trouillot riding in the same old, ugly, black Mercedes-Benz that Papa Doc used. I was on Avenue John Brown in Port-au-Prince, where piles of trash forced her driver to swerve the car to keep from running over street vendors. A vendor told me she passed along the smelly street every day at the same time on her way to the National Palace. The Mercedes-Benz with the license plate number — 22 22 — brought back many bad memories. It looked like a hearse carrying a corpse to the cemetery. I remembered how Francois Duvalier, especially during national holidays, rode through the capital city, throwing coins in the streets to the needy. Some of the people were killed by Papa Doc's convoy in the scramble to pick up a few dimes and pennies. Once, I saw a car in the convoy hit and kill a young boy on Boulevard Jean

Jacques Dessalines near St. Jean Bosco church, former President Jean-Bertrand Aristide's old church. He had one gourde — 20 cents — in his hand. His body, swarmed by mosquitoes, lay in the street for hours. People were afraid to look at the body because Francois Duvalier and his agents of death, the personal militia known as the Tonton Macoutes, controlled the people with fear.

The Tonton Macoutes dressed in heavy blue uniforms with red scarves around their necks and machetes slung on their hips. They paraded in the streets ready to butcher innocent people like animals in a slaughterhouse. "Dead men don't talk" was the Macoutes' motto.

Papa Doc chose a commander for each popular neighborhood. In my neighborhood, Francois Louisol, also known as Boss Pint, was the commander. I grew up five houses down from Louisol's political office. As a young boy, I saw the notorious Louisol kill and abuse many people. My father, St. Louis Regis, was terrified after Macoutes killed my uncle Mirabeau Alexandre, my mother's brother. Two weeks later, they arrested her other brother, Uncle Nicolas, and sent him to the infamous military barracks called Fort Dimanche, where many innocent people were imprisoned. It was a human butcher shop owned and operated by torturers licensed by Papa Doc to commit atrocities. My father's best friend was a Tonton Macoute who advised my father to enroll in their terrorist group for his protection. Fortunately, the district commander denied my father's application. He accused my father of wanting to become a Macoute to avenge his brother-in-law's death.

A few months passed before my father was arrested by another friend who had become a Macoute. But my father's life was spared. His friend asked the authorities to release my father as a favor because he was innocent.

Francois Duvalier made us believe he had the power to disappear, or turn himself into a guinea hen, which was his symbol. Papa Doc's political opponents gave up after they failed to overthrow him several times. They were waiting like a bunch of shoeless men wait for a dead man's shoes, but Papa Doc passed his shoes to his son in front of us. We were still afraid of Papa Doc even when he died. Because we thought Papa Doc was immortal, we were afraid to say he was dead. I don't know why I thought of all these things when I saw Pascal-Trouillot ride by in that hearse.

Maybe Pascal-Trouillot was looking for good luck from the barons of Duvalier. Twenty-two was Duvalier's so-called magic number, and he held all important events on the 22nd of the month. In my mind, the presidential car affirmed Pascal-Trouillot's association with Duvalier. She seemed to support the same corrupt system we fought hard to forget, the stubborn 29-year-old scar the cannibal regime left on the face of our nation that we fought hard to erase. But my mother disagreed with me, and claimed Pascal-Trouillot tried her best to unite the leadership.

When I returned to Haiti again in February 1996, I told a friend of mine that I would like to meet the ex-president and talk to her about her political past. It was difficult to find her because she lives an obscure life and many people had forgotten about her. My wife, Franki, and I eventually found her house and stopped by unexpectedly. We were surprised at how freely she talked with us about Haiti's deadly road to democracy. It was Feb. 6, 1996, one day before Aristide passed power to his protégé Rene Preval, Haiti's current president.

After hours of interviewing her, I concluded that she probably had some blood on her hands, because Haiti is a land of corruption. No one is innocent, not even the members of the clergy who are supposed to be the voice of the poor. I do understand she had to deal with people who conspired to force her out of office. I was impressed with how well she stood up against her opponents, and how determined she was to hold presidential elections. But her resistance to the opposition killed any chance of a future political career, and that suited Pascal-Trouillot just fine.

On our first visit to her home, Pascal-Trouillot didn't look the part of a conniving politician. She wore spectacles and a simple print dress, and her hair was pulled back in her trademark bun. Her youthful looks were fading. She looked almost old, but she refused to say how old she was. Reflecting on her presidential days, she conceded she was happy to hand power to Aristide.

The election was the best thing for Haiti, she said. "The president and staff were ready to give up power. It was a very heavy load to carry. One year seemed like 10 years of hard labor."

A women's activist, Pascal-Trouillot is the author of several books, including "The Judicial Status of Haitian Women in Social Legislation." Another book, "On the Grand Boulevard of Liberty," is her account of the U.S. legal system after she visited America in 1980. She now spends her days writing law books and traveling around the world participating in conferences on women and law issues. She lives in the heart of Port-au-Prince, where vendors selling goods squat outside the iron gate surrounding her yellow home. "The vendors have nowhere to go," she said, when asked why she allows the vendors to sell outside her home. "In Haiti life is bizarre. I could be in their place."

Looking around her home, I didn't see any signs of a lavish lifestyle. An old typewriter and a small fax machine sat on a desk. As past president, the Haitian government pays her 7,500 gourdes a month, which is equivalent to $1,500 in American money. Two old Toyotas were on the grounds. Franki and I were interviewing her when the government conducted its daily electricity shutdown to conserve energy, forcing us to write under the flicker of oil lamps. Pascal-Trouillot said she couldn't afford a generator, laughing as she recalled how opposition leaders accused her of emptying the government coffers. The country was broke when she took power, she said, because previous leaders had fled with millions.

On Saturdays, Pascal-Trouillot spends a great deal of time in church. She is a Seventh-Day Adventist; while president, she was Roman Catholic, but because of the bad treatment she said she received from Aristide, a former Catholic priest, she changed her religious denomination.

Pascal-Trouillot grew up in Petionville, a suburb of Port-au-Prince, with nine siblings in a middle-class family. There were rumors that she was not well off because people said her father was an ironmonger who died when she was young. Some said her mother earned a living as a washerwoman.

I must admit that many Haitians sometimes say they grew up middle class, although they were dirt poor. The middle class doesn't exist in Haiti, but the poor often put themselves in classes based on degrees of poverty, and think they are better off than others if they can afford food, clothing and education. Even in suburban Petionville, mansions and shacks are side by side. But people like to say they live in Petionville because it makes them appear better than the majority. When my brother Andre sent a few dollars from the United States back to my family, we moved to a different neighborhood so it would appear that we were doing better financially; in reality, we were still just as poor as we always were. We brought all the raggedy furniture we had in the old house when we moved. The truth is the majority of Haitians have relatives who live abroad and send money back for necessities. I don't know if this was the case with Pascal-Trouillot.

Pascal-Trouillot said she attended private schools and graduated at the top of her classes. Her whole family, except her, emigrated to New York in late 1960 after one of the Tonton Macoutes, under Papa Doc, shot her youngest brother Alix in the back, permanently paralyzing him.

Pascal-Trouillot, who has never lived outside Haiti, has one adult daughter who attended college and now lives in the United States. Pascal-Trouillot practiced law alongside her late husband, with whom she co-authored a book, "The Code of Common Laws." She had dreamed of becoming a doctor, but during college her future husband, then president of the Port-au-Prince bar at the time, persuaded her to go to law school. She graduated from the Gonaives Law School in 1971, and later became a civil court judge before her appointment to the Supreme Court.

The Department of Justice didn't reinstate Pascal-Trouillot to her judgeship after she left the presidency. She had four years left on her 10-year term on the Supreme Court. A political outsider after she left politics, she stayed that way.

"This is the Haitian way," she said. "People forget about you if you can't do anything for them. People need jobs and money. I was too serious; a strong, powerful woman. They wanted a puppet. Haiti, a chauvinist nation, wasn't ready for a woman president."

After my wife and I left Pascal-Trouillot's house, we talked about the many bad things we had heard and read about her. She seemed the opposite in person: honest, open, friendly, not the cold, calculating, power-hungry lawyer many people said she was. She seemed content with her simple life.

Before we left the country, we asked many people their opinion of Madame Pascal-Trouillot. In Haiti, a country where

85 percent of the population is illiterate, rumors are rampant and news by word of mouth travels quickly. Haitians were divided in their opinions of Pascal-Trouillot. Some said she was a corrupt leader willing to do anything to maintain power. Others described her as a competent president.

We went to talk to the Rev. Roger Desire, an Episcopal priest. When he met us at the door, I was expecting to see a younger man because his voice sounded so powerful on the telephone. He was tall, of medium build with white hair. His voice, passionate when he talked about Aristide, turned angry when asked to describe Pascal-Trouillot. "She was a de facto president," said Desire, who was active in the Lavalas movement. "Her administration was infested with corruption. She was walking on a land mine."

Others said her presidential appointment violated the constitution, which, in Haiti, is a piece of paper that is mutilated daily. Leslie Jean, a government employee during Pascal-Trouillot's term, said she was a crook who had political opponents killed. A popular radio journalist we talked to one evening in her stuffy, hot office went as far to say that she believed Pascal-Trouillot illegally tried to maintain power by staging a coup. Lilianne Pierre Paul, co-owner of Radio Kiskeya, said although she believes Pascal-Trouillot was involved in the coup, she was a good administrator who "was the first one to open the door to democracy."

My mother never criticized Pascal-Trouillot despite the accusations of corruption, murder, incompetence and favoritism. Her government, my mother said, in collaboration with the United States, was responsible for Haiti's first free and democratic election on Dec. 16, 1990. ◗

Peasants stand in line
waiting to cast
their votes
for democracy.

Henchmen stand in line
armed-to-the-teeth
waiting to cast
their votes
for terrorism.

A VOTE FOR DEMOCRACY

My mother, like most Haitians, was conditioned not to vote during elections, even after she had the opportunity to exercise her right. She assumed that after decades of institutional oppression and repression, an election would not bring democracy to a country without structure. She was an eyewitness to violence that surrounded past unlawful elections.

However, on Dec. 16, 1990, the government didn't bus voters from the countryside to Port-au-Prince. It did not force them to vote several times, as they did when the Duvaliers were in power. Long gone were the days when Francois "Papa Doc" Duvalier amended the so-called constitution that declared him president for life.

But history has a way of repeating itself, my mother recalled, as it did in 1988 when the military rigged the presidential election that put into power moderate conservative Leslie Manigat. He was toppled four months later in a military coup d'état.

I tried to convince my mother that things were different. How could things be better when the brutal military still existed? she asked. Deep down I knew she was speaking from a life of experience, but I categorically rejected her beliefs. I and most Haitians were focused on the election. We believed that after the election all of Haiti's problems would be resolved. I was eager to cast my vote and be a part of history in the making.

I was not in Haiti during that historic election, for I was a photo intern at the Los Angeles Times. I was despondent that I was unable to participate in my country's first democratic election. After years of rigged votes, I finally had the chance to vote in a free election and I wasn't in my homeland to do so.

A few weeks before the election, Jean Glouis, a friend who lives in Miami, sent me a list of the presidential candidates. I wasn't surprised when I saw a total of 11 names. In Haiti, the only qualification for a presidential candidate is that he owns a house in that country. It is why we have so many unqualified candidates.

Still, I had never voted in my life and wanted to feel the power of my vote. I held a mock election in my bedroom in Los Angeles on Dec. 16, 1990. I wrote profiles for each Haitian presidential candidate based on their qualifications, background and platform. I disqualified five of the 11 candidates before I began voting.

The six leading candidates were Thomas Desulme, a businessman whose name I crossed out; the late Louis Dejoie, Jr., who also didn't get my vote; Hubert de Ronceray, a sociologist and demagogue, who was eliminated; Marc Bazin, the United States choice, who also didn't make the cut; and the late Silvio Claude, who lived in my neighborhood and was a Baptist minister who became a martyr for the poor during the Duvalier regime. He had no chance to win.

Finally, I voted for Jean-Bertrand Aristide, because he was one of the few who defended our rights even at the risk of his life. He was one of us, a son of a peasant who struggled to survive just like us. He was someone who could understand our plight, our suffering and our tribulation, because he grew up in a shanty like 95 percent of the population. My mother loved Father Aristide. She went to his church, St. Jean Bosco, every morning, but she never put her faith in him as president. In Haiti, she said, it's

"every man for himself."

Francois Duvalier grew up poor. And what did he do for Haiti? Nothing, besides bankrupt the country and kill innocent people. Yet my mother and I weren't looking at the situation in Haiti through the same magnifying glass. She had lived through the history she told me about and of which I had learned from books at school. She used to say, "Experience surpasses science." Although she was illiterate, my mother was an intelligent woman who knew much about her homeland. But I blindly supported Aristide, and believed he was the best candidate for Haiti.

While I analyzed the situation miles away through rose-colored glasses in Los Angeles, the poor voters in Haiti gathered early before the polling places opened. Some waited for hours to cast their votes for president, members of parliament, and mayors. During elections, the majority of voters depend on photographs of each candidate to help them choose one by marking an X by the candidate's name. The people were determined to make sure their votes counted.

Pascal-Trouillot also went to the polls early to register her vote. She wanted to reassure the population that this election was free of violence. She didn't vote for a presidential candidate, but did cast her ballot for two friends who ran for senator. As I listened to live election returns via telephone from my friend in Miami, I thought of my grandfather, who died at age 80. He never had the chance to vote. My father, who died at age 63, also never voted. The word "vote" was never spoken in our house because in Haiti, certain words are banished from your vocabulary for your own safety. My family members could have been killed for expressing their opinions with such words. "Communist." "Election." "Democracy," "vote," "candidate" and "unemployment." "Abuse" and "hunger."

Nevertheless, I wished my mother would have voted and said all those words out loud for my late father, and especially for me. I never had the chance to vote or say those words publicly in Haiti. I was disappointed with her decision not to participate in that historic event, but I understood her unwillingness. I remembered how on Nov. 27, 1987, soldiers massacred more than 30 of my countrymen who showed up at the polls to vote. Maybe my mother had flashbacks on election day in 1990, for one of the victims of the 1987 slaughter had lived in her neighborhood.

On Dec. 16, 1990, I kept in constant contact with my friend in Miami. He put his telephone receiver on his radio speaker so I could hear election results transmitted directly from Haiti. Before the polls closed, Aristide supporters took to the streets, celebrating his victory. I suspect this was a tactic that Aristide's political party used to prevent fraud by Duvalier thugs.

Aristide was a political wild card. When he entered politics, he didn't have a political party or a platform. But he was the only one who could stop the country from falling into the hands of a Duvalierist, or a puppet of the bourgeoisie. Less than two months before the election, some political parties combined to create the Front National for Change and Democracy, the FNCD, which supported Father Aristide.

The election, witnessed by international observers from the United States, United Nations and the Organization of American States, was declared Haiti's first honest and peaceful election. Jean-Bertrand Aristide, a Roman Catholic priest popular in the slums, an outspoken critic of the younger Duvalier, the bourgeoisie, and the church hierarchy, had been elected president by a landslide. After the election I believed that things were going to get better. I believed that Haitians had finally chosen a true representative of the people.

My mother told me that the election was a rehearsal for democracy; it wasn't a vote for true democracy. I was pleased to see the proletariat finally take control of the country when they elected a president, senators, representatives and mayors. I had always believed that for Haiti to move forward, its leaders must come from the people who had suffered, been abused and jailed.

Aristide was elected president of Haiti without campaigning. He didn't even debate the other leading candidates. This is Haiti, a land where anything goes. He had less than two months to prepare for his five-year term, a big challenge for someone who decided to run for the highest office of the land at the last minute. Although he is a powerful speaker, I knew that words alone couldn't change the sad state of my country. He was a priest from the Salesian order who probably never balanced a budget even for himself. I wondered how he could change Haiti. ❱

III

We called him savior
because we believed
and trusted him
as the only man
who would lead Haiti
down the road to democracy.

FATHER OF DEMOCRACY

My mother sat quietly on her porch on Feb. 7, 1991, while provisional president Ertha Pascal-Trouillot handed over power to Jean-Bertrand Aristide, the president-elect. My mother didn't join the crowd in front of the Legislative Palace or the National Palace to witness the history-making event. She sat close to her radio and listened to the "father of democracy" make promises during his inauguration speech, promises that would go unfulfilled.

The transfer of power from Pascal-Trouillot to Aristide represented the end of the Duvalier dynasty. For most Haitians, Feb. 7 stands for more than the downfall of Jean-Claude Duvalier. It symbolizes hope for a better Haiti, and justice for the people tired of being beaten, abused and killed by a savage military regime.

I believe most poor Haitians thought on Feb. 7, 1991, that Aristide would resolve our problems that run deep, to Haiti's colonial history of slavery. We knew our burdens were a lot to saddle upon the president of a country that is the poorest in the Western Hemisphere. Disregarding statistics, we put our faith in Aristide, because during the bad times he always stood with us. Yet our faith in Aristide was an illusion. We knew we were dreaming, but it felt so good, we didn't want to wake up.

Weeks before Aristide's inauguration, his supporters in the Lavalas, the popular grass-roots movement he formed, worked day and night giving the country a face lift. They cleaned streets and picked up all the trash; they didn't want their president taking power in an office surrounded by filth. This was a rare occasion where the majority of Haitians joined in neighborhood watch groups to protect each other from the paramilitary.

There were parties throughout the country as people waited for inauguration day. They danced their misery away in the streets. Some walked in the dark, holding lighted candles while others sang, "Haiti is free at last."

Historically, Haiti has always been in transition. The most recent change was from a brutal Duvalier regime to a succession of military governments that hired attachés and "zenglendo" — thugs — to carry out a reign of terror. But in this, the latest transition to come to Haiti, Aristide raised his right hand at the Legislative Palace and solemnly declared:

"I swear before God and before the nation that I will respect the constitution and the laws of the country and I will make everyone follow them."

It was a pledge that made the people happy, for that day was a new beginning for them. It represented an end to their enslavement, not by French masters, but by fellow countrymen who for nearly three decades ruled the country with an iron fist. A handful of wealthy families and dictators have marred the country in political struggles, and shed blood over money and power. The bourgeois are reluctant to vote; they know they are in the minority and that their money can buy the election of a president. If, however, the president doesn't want to be a puppet, he will most likely be killed or overthrown by the military — in a

coup funded by the bourgeois. Aristide preached against the bourgeoisie and the capitalists, especially the United States, from the pulpit in his church, St. Jean Bosco. His church would be the springboard for building his political machine.

Meanwhile, Pascal-Trouillot said she was eager to remove the heavy load from her back and transfer power to Aristide. She said Aristide considered her a traitor because of an unsuccessful coup attempt one month before he was sworn into office. The late Roger Lafontant, a notorious Macoute, took Pascal-Trouillot hostage for 10 hours on Dec. 7, 1990. Lafontant, a Duvalierist, former interior minister under Jean-Claude Duvalier and longtime associate of Francois Duvalier, declared himself president. In response, thousands of Haitians flooded the streets of Port-au-Prince in protest. Aristide supporters set tires on fire and barricaded streets. Dozens of people were killed before the military, under the leadership of General Herard Abraham, arrested Lafontant and put a stop to the uprising. Although Pascal-Trouillot announced on national television that she was forced to resign, Aristide still believed she was involved in the conspiracy against his government. I also believed at the time that she was the mastermind behind the coup, or was somehow involved.

Behind this backdrop, Aristide's inauguration wasn't pleasant. Pascal-Trouillot said guests impatiently waited for Aristide, who was more than two hours late. He also excluded her from the ceremony; in clear view of attendants, Aristide sent her a letter that she refused to accept. Before he was sworn in, Aristide invited a peasant, instead of Pascal-Trouillot, to place the presidential sash around his shoulder. It appeared to be a symbolic gesture for the country, a powerful statement from a president who had obtained power from poor constituents instead of the rich bourgeois, the ruling class that had fixed elections in the past.

Aristide was so eager to condemn Pascal-Trouillot that the next day he had the letter delivered to her home. He accused her in the letter of taking part in the failed coup d'état. Aristide took justice in his own hands like the people who took to the streets protesting. Pascal-Trouillot said Aristide should have set an example for the people as the head of the nation. Instead, she said, he was a "chef de bande" — a poor leader.

A few days later, Pascal-Trouillot was arrested at her home — she said there was no warrant — and jailed at Caserne Dessalines, a military barracks behind the National Palace. My mother was very upset about Pascal-Trouillot's arrest. She recalled how the Tonton Macoutes arrested her brother, Nicolas Remy. He spent two years and four months as a prisoner at the Fort Dimanche military barracks. He was one of the few survivors of the Haitian death camp.

Pascal-Trouillot said Aristide had her arrested with the intention of allowing a mob to break into the jail, drag her out, and burn her in front of the National Palace. Yet the former Madame President spent only one day in jail. While we were happy she was incarcerated, the international community put pressure on Aristide to release her.

"He had to swallow his pride and let me go," Pascal-Trouillot said. "I was unharmed, unlike others whom Aristide disliked." She added that Aristide later came to her home and apologized for his treatment of her.

Aristide, who had no political background, a common trait among Haiti's politicians, was beset by criticism in the early stages of his presidency. His critics accused him of using the same tactics his predecessors used in persuading followers to attack the opposition. They accused Aristide of encouraging supporters to put burning tires around the necks of opponents. During the presidential address at the National Palace, Aristide instructed General Abraham to fire a group of officers that Aristide considered too old to serve in the military. It would be the president's first big mistake, one that would cost him a mountain of grief. By alienating the army, Aristide took the risk thinking that the people would support him. He forgot that the poor had no guns.

Aristide named Rene Preval prime minister. During the first seven months of Aristide's administration, the country wasn't as politically and economically sound as the government propaganda proclaimed to the international community. Aristide and his coalition party, the FNCD, had no vision for Haiti. Their platform was merely talk and no action. They did nothing to feed poor Haitians who saw Aristide as a prophet sent by God to save

Haiti.

The popular government spent a great deal of time seeking revenge from people with money and power, rather than working with them to help the country go forward. Lacking political experience, Aristide took the wrong approach. He directed the majority population to take justice into its own hands, because the country's justice system was destroyed by the corrupt Duvalier dynasty and five years of military rule. Aristide claimed to be the voice of the people, just as the Duvalierists had done. In a nation of which 85 percent of the population is illiterate, he played on the political ignorance of the masses.

Haiti's peasant class has been a doormat for the bourgeoisie since the country's independence from the French in 1804, as well as for political leaders who step on the heads of the peasants. Aristide's government failed to do anything constructive for its people during his seven months in power. The poor got poorer. The cost of living in the country, which imported almost 90 percent of its goods and exported nothing, increased.

Yet the people still believed things would get better. Haiti had been ruled for so long by dictators that the people and their elected officials have no conception of what democracy means. Everyone's eyes were on Aristide to see what he would do. Instead of helping him plant the seed of democracy, they took a wait-and-see approach. Unfortunately, the masses fought in vain with their vote and their lives to end Macoutism.

Just because a democratic president is elected doesn't necessarily mean the country is ruled democratically. The president, eager to show his supporters he meant business, made many preparatory errors. He governed the country as if he were running St. Jean Bosco church. When he said something he expected everybody to bow down and kiss his feet.

On Sept. 30, 1991, the rumor of a coup against the new president would become a reality. Aristide, the popular yet flawed leader that a nation's poor would put their hopes for democracy upon, was overthrown in a bloody coup d'état under the leadership of Lieutenant General Raoul Cedras. ▶

IV

Another coup,
that expunged the last hope
for penniless Haitians.

Another coup,
that made fathers and mothers
weep on the graves
of their innocent sons and daughters.

Another coup,
that transposed the leaders
of the Lavalas movement into clans,
power hungry and corrupt.

Another coup,
a brutal coup that opened
Haiti's old wounds.

ANOTHER COUP

My mother was right to allow the family's nonvoting tradition to stand. The military did not fix the presidential election, yet it overthrew Aristide in a bloody coup d'état after he had served only seven months. In his seven months in power, Aristide attempted to clean up public administration, to reform the military, and to stop the use of Haiti as a transshipment point for smuggling cocaine. The coup that ousted him changed the president's life forever as well as the lives of Haitians. Although Aristide's life was spared, he left behind a bloody trail of innocent people killed by the military and its goons in the name of democracy.

Military leaders who Aristide had appointed worked in conjunction with the bourgeois who financed the coup. Among the architects of the coup was Lieutenant General Raoul Cedras, who served as interim military commander while Aristide was in power. When the military goons stormed Aristide's residence on Sept. 30, 1991, he had been aware that there was a plot against his administration but also believed the masses would take to the streets and protect him. They protested when Roger Lafontant tried to seize power from Ertha Pascal-Trouillot and keep Aristide from taking office. Aristide's situation reminded me of the Haitian proverb, "malfini manke ou, li pa bliye ou" — "the vulture missed you, but it didn't forget you." The military did not forget Aristide, and pulled the plug that caused a political, social and economic blackout in the country.

I was angry, but I wasn't surprised.

I later found out that while most of the people slept, armed thugs left the military academy, killing anyone who ventured in their path as they headed toward the neighborhood of Tabarre, where Aristide lived. Soldiers approaching the president's house in an army tank began shooting. Witnesses said Aristide escaped in an armored car of the French ambassador Jean Raphaél Dufour to the National Palace, where he was arrested. Gunshots were heard outside the Palace. Witnesses recalled a soldier put a tire — pé lebrun — around Aristide's neck and demanded gasoline and matches. This was apparently in retaliation for the times when Aristide, after he was elected, encouraged his supporters to put burning tires around the necks of his opponents. Aristide denied he ever encouraged anyone to do that.

"No," another soldier said. "Let me shoot him."

But the majority wanted Aristide alive, but sent into exile. Witnesses who recalled the scenario said Aristide lowered his head and closed his eyes. A soldier came toward him and told him to open his eyes. "You are not going to disappear the same way you did at St. Jean Bosco Church," he said, referring to the time military attachés stormed Aristide's church and tried to kill him. Parishioners threw their bodies over the diminutive former priest, saving his life.

But there was no one to rescue the frail, terrified president at the palace that night. The coup participants had killed Captain Fritz Pierre Louis, Aristide's bodyguard, who stood behind him at the palace. The soldiers broke Aristide's eyeglasses, shoved and beat him. Although they threatened to kill him, they ended up taking him to army headquarters where Cedras and his clan waited. There, they forced Aristide to write and sign a letter of resignation. I often wonder what Aristide was thinking while he signed away the presidency that his supporters had given him. I imagined he shook like a leaf and asked for forgiveness.

The rumor mill said Cedras and the others poked fun at Aristide at first. Cedras said that he had appointed himself president. After the joking ended, lengthy negotiations involving the fate of the popular president began. American Ambassador Alvin Adams, and the Haitian military Colonel Alix Silva, pleaded with the coup leaders to send Aristide into exile instead of killing him. The military escorted Aristide and Dufour to Port-au-Prince International Airport. It was about 1 a.m. when Aristide fled the country on a flight to Caracas, Venezuela, under Dufour's protection.

The airplane carrying Aristide landed at Caracas International Airport two hours later. Shortly after arriving in Caracas, Aristide traveled to Washington, D.C., to meet with representatives from the Organization of American States. He also met with then-President George Bush, members of the Congressional Black Caucus, and the Commission on Human Rights.

Meanwhile in Haiti, Cedras proclaimed himself commander in chief of the army. His action reminded me of the Haitian proverb, "Joumou pa donnen kalbas" — "Squash cannot produce calabash." The country was once again in chaos, similar to the dark days when "Papa Doc" and his feared Tonton Macoutes ruled. The army took over the streets, especially in poor neighborhoods that were political strongholds of Aristide. To silence Aristide's supporters, military attachés murdered them. Each morning, dead bodies lined the streets. The military's coup against justice and democracy had succeeded. They would celebrate by torturing and killing more innocent people.

At a time when the people needed their leaders the most, they were unavailable to help the people bear the cross of tribulation handed to them by their own brothers. Most of the so-called leaders fled when the people who voted them into office needed them the most. Some politicians exchanged their leadership roles for U.S. visas while death squads murdered their supporters. The people were left behind, their lives exposed to peril. The leaders who stayed in Haiti hoarded fortunes at the expense of the needy.

My heart ached for my people. I wondered if those military cowards, who also had families, had a collective conscience. My tiny Caribbean country was like a snake without a head; anyone with a gun had power.

It seemed poor Haitians were born to suffer all their lives. The de facto government abused them without mercy. Anyone who sought justice faced a losing battle. The army killed men and raped women. They beat the elderly. No one was exempt, except the thugs' own family members. If the military brutes did not value the lives of their own people, how were we to expect them to respect the constitution? The role of Supreme Court justices is to interpret the constitution. Yet in Haiti, blinded by greed and power, they aided the military thugs in breaking the law by installing illegal governments. The 1987 constitution was just a piece of paper without value.

On Oct. 8, 1991, the military gave Aristide's government the coup de grace by installing Supreme Court Justice Joseph Nerette as provisional president. Jean Jacques Honorat, a human rights activist, took over as prime minister to succeed Rene Preval. The unconstitutional, de facto regime governed with the support of a parliamentary majority and the armed forces until Nerette and Honorat resigned in June 1992. The Parliament, also with the support of the armed forces, approved Marc Bazin as prime minister to head a new de facto government; a presidential replacement wasn't named. Aristide, the candidate of the masses, had crushed Bazin, the U.S.-backed candidate, during the presidential elections. But the humiliated United States learned how to play the complicated political game of Haitian politics. In Haiti, presidents are elected directly by the people, not by a college of electoral votes as in the United States. Popularity, not money, counts in Haiti.

Bazin's role was to negotiate a solution with Aristide, the president in exile, as well as an end to the economic embargo and diplomatic isolation of Haiti imposed after Aristide's ouster. Yet

Bazin resigned a year later, and the United Nations imposed oil and arms embargoes that forced the Haitian military to the negotiating table.

Since Haiti's independence, most of its presidents were removed or installed by the military. In May 1994, the military, conspiring with Parliament, installed Supreme Court Justice Emile Jonassaint as provisional president. The lawmakers broke the laws for money, for, as we say in Creole, "Lajan fé chin dansé" — "Money makes dogs dance." During that time so-called leaders of the poor gorged themselves, and they're still eating.

Haiti had parallel governments. The illegitimate military-backed Jonassaint regime controlled the national government, which prevented the constitutionally backed government-in-exile from carrying out its duties. Parliament also had parallel leadership in the Senate that mirrored the dual governments, and was unable to function effectively.

As a result, the United Nations tightened its economic embargo on Haiti. In late July 1994, the international community suspended all commercial airline flights to Haiti. In addition, the United Nations adopted a resolution authorizing member states to use all necessary means to facilitate the departure of Haiti's military leadership and restore constitutional rule. ❭

Somebody, please rescue me.
I am fleeing repression.

Somebody, please rescue me.
You see my painful tragedy,
don't close your eyes.

Somebody, please rescue me.
I have nothing to offer
but my hunger for democracy.

Somebody, please rescue me.
You know I am poor
and from a country with no oil.

Somebody, please rescue me.
You heard the voice of Kuwait
all the way from the desert.
Why can't you hear my voice
in your backyard?

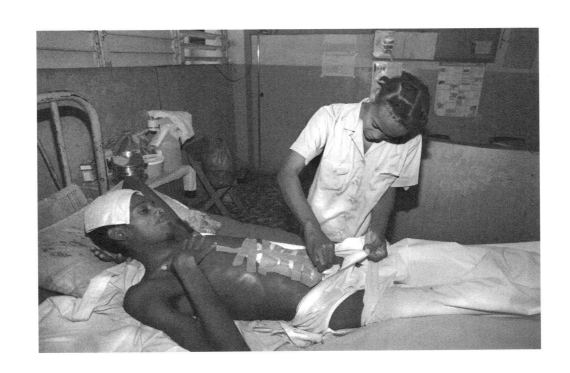

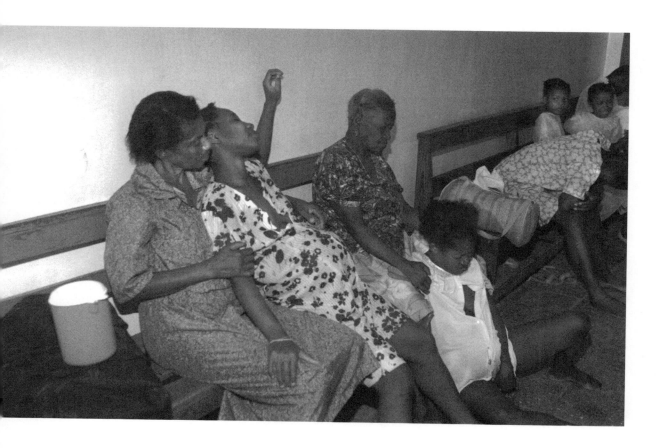

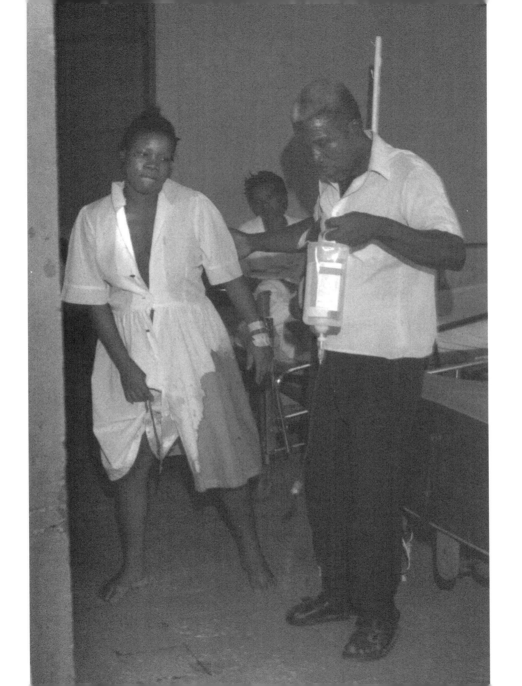

51

ARISTIDE IN EXILE

My mother laughed when I told her the U.N.-led embargo was supposed to bring Haitian military leaders to their knees. She was wiser than me in assessing that it had only destabilized the struggle of Haitian people. An embargo always hurts the masses because they have no one to turn to for help. The elite had visas they used to travel to America, Europe or Canada to buy whatever goods they needed.

My mother saw the fake embargo as a ploy to devastate the poor who had survived more than three decades of abuse, hunger and murder under the Duvaliers. My mother had never been outside of Haiti and spoke from her life's experiences. She had a small business selling rice, beans and oil. She sold on credit because few of her regular customers had money to buy necessities. When she died, she left a scribbled list of names of customers who owed her a total of 10,000 gourdes.

My mother feared for her life during the reign of the military troops, who killed people in broad daylight as hunters would shoot birds. She was also afraid that someone would kill Aristide while he was in exile because he criticized the American government. My mother thought all other nations were like Haiti, where you may be killed for criticizing a president or his government. She believed Aristide would never return to his native country, or be assassinated if he set foot on his native soil.

It was risky for me to travel to Haiti during the military rule, but I found myself on an airplane in November 1992 after the death of my mother.

My youngest sister was visiting from New York when we got a late-night telephone call from my brother who lives in Miami. Someone had telephoned him from Haiti with the sad news that our mother had passed away. It was imperative for me to pay my respects to a woman who had never learned to read or write, but was able to feed, clothe and educate six children in a country where the average income is about $3 a day. My mother never got the chance to live her life to the fullest. Her dream was for me, my sisters and my brother to have a life of luxury.

I feel a bit of exuberance because we now live in a country where people have the opportunity to send their children to school, to eat every day, and to live in comfortable homes. I was going by plane to a country, my country, where most people eat sometime. Most of them never go to school, and many are homeless, including a growing number of children. They sleep among the mounds of stinky trash piled in the streets. The homeless fight with the roaming goats and dogs for a morsel of food that may be buried among the garbage. Women and girls on the way from the markets carry heavy baskets of goods upon their heads. Men push heavy loads of items in old, creaky wheelbarrows

Beggars are everywhere. They are the first to greet you at the airport. Some stand at the entrance of restaurants and beg for scraps of food, and employees chase them away with broom handles. A few are educated, most are not. They come in all shapes and sizes. Some are crippled. Some are young, some are old. Some are women dragging snotty-nosed babies behind them. They constantly follow you down the street begging for money.

Home for people who are fortunate to have one is usually a one-room shanty with no electricity or indoor plumbing. When I was a child, my parents slept in the one bed and the six kids slept on the floor. In the morning, we got a cup of water and went outside to wash our bodies and brush our teeth. The sanitation system is poor, and women carry buckets of water on their heads to sell on the streets. For breakfast, we usually had a cup of coffee and some biscuit dough. Dinner was most likely rice and beans. On Sundays, if we were lucky, we had chicken. My parents got the meatier pieces, the thighs. The two oldest children got one leg each. The other sister got the neck, and I got one foot. This is typical family life in Haiti.

The Haiti I arrived in was on the verge of civil unrest. Everyone was leader, lawyer, judge and jury. I was frightened when the immigration agent took my passport and opened an old notebook glued upon a big piece of wood. Francois Duvalier established this procedure to keep "communists" from entering the country. I shook with fear as the immigration agent flipped page after handwritten yellow page, for I had good reason to be scared. Three years earlier my half-brother Rousseau, who never left Haiti, was killed by the military during the fight for freedom and justice. I did not go to his funeral because the country was under martial law. What would happen to me if he found my name in the old notebook? I thought. I didn't know anyone in Haiti who could help me. I couldn't even call a lawyer or post bond if I was arrested. What a shame. I was lost in my thoughts when the agent said, "You are clear," and returned my passport.

I was shocked by the poverty that gripped Haiti after Aristide's ouster. Things had gotten worse. I was ready to share what I had with the people because my mother taught us to share with others.

"A hungry man is an angry man," she used to say.

I saw hopelessness in the faces of my people. This could have been my life. I grew up with them, played with them, ate with them. The only difference was that God blessed me by helping me escape to the United States. But it was difficult for the poor to flee Haiti at that time, for U.S. military boats were stationed off the coast to return anyone trying to leave.

I stayed in Haiti for 10 days, and entered places where I was not allowed to go when I grew up there. I went to some million-dollar homes where rulers of the country lived. They were decorated with imported furniture from the U.S. and Europe. Shiny luxury cars and sports-utility vehicles were parked in the driveways. I revisited tin shacks in the poverty-stricken neighborhood where I grew up. In some, more than 10 lived in a single room. When it rained, water accumulated in their homes. The only assets the parents had were their children.

The disparity was shameful. I always heard that the country is divided into two categories, but this was the first time I visited the other side. I finally understood why the bourgeoisie fought hard with terror and exploitation to keep their privileges.

The devastation I saw made me curious to see what shape the hospitals were in since the embargo was imposed. I visited General Hospital, a facility that serves about 80 percent of the Port-au-Prince population. The conditions at the hospital were always deficient, but with the embargo, the penniless had it more difficult. Relatives are responsible to feed, bathe, clothe and buy medicine for patients.

I saw a male patient with a dingy intravenous fluid bag connected to his arm; he was screaming, "The pain is too much." The smell of the man's waste permeated the doors of the therapeutic building. A woman standing nearby attempted to calm him because there were no doctors or nurses present.

In comparison, when the elite fell ill, they simply flew to Miami for treatment.

Yet the poor still believed Father Aristide was a prophet sent from God to change the country so everyone would have, as in Aristide's own words, "a seat around the table." While Aristide was in exile, traveling with his entourage around the world, his hungry supporters never gave up hope. They were willing to die for him because they believed he was the only president who could change their lives. The longer he was in exile, the louder the people he left behind called for his return. Mutilated and tortured bodies found on roadsides each morning didn't silence the cries from his supporters in the slums, Aristide's strong political base. Thousands of people lost their lives. In Port-au-Prince and the countryside, repression reached its peak.

"No Aristide, No Peace," they chanted.

As the pressure mounted, many took refuge in nearby Santo Domingo or other Caribbean islands. Others risked their lives on small rickety boats, trying to reach south Florida. Thousands died on their way to America, never reaching the "Promised Land" as their families waited in vain to hear from them. The ones who made it were sent directly to the hot, dusty, fenced-in barracks at Guantanamo Bay, the United States military base in Cuba. Others were returned to Haiti, where they faced firing squads.

The Bush administration wasn't fond of Aristide. It did little to help restore the leftist priest to power, or stop the slaughter in Haiti. The embargo was the idea of the Organization of American States, yet the U.S. government later jumped on board for political reasons. It did not make a good-faith effort to resolve the problems of a country that had nothing to trade but misery. Haiti is not oil-rich Kuwait.

Although the embargo caused the poor to suffer, they still rallied for Father Aristide. Haiti became more dependent on foreign charity that never reached the needy. Military leaders got richer selling on the black market. The embargo created more millionaires in Haiti than 29 years of corruption did under Duvalier. The embargo would in time be used as a weapon to force the poor to forget Aristide. Peasants died of malnutrition while caravans of trucks bursting with rice, beans and gasoline made their way from neighboring Dominican Republic to Port-au-Prince, the capital of corruption.

Haiti's borders opened as a free enterprise zone for contraband, especially drugs. There was a place in Port-au-Prince the people called Kuwait City, because oil tankers from the Dominican Republic stopped there and sold barrels of oil. Gas was sold on the street like food because gas stations were closed. Most of the country's legitimate national businesses shut down and the country's dependence on American goods increased. I'm sure that was the idea behind the deceptive embargo.

My mother was right when she said the embargo was a way to destroy the national product. The poor became poorer. Thousands died from an involuntary hunger strike. But they never turned against Aristide. Haitian military leaders miscalculated the effect of an embargo because it did not drive the wolves out of the woods.

They still cried, "No Aristide, No Peace."

The U.S. government grew impatient with pro-Aristide supporters and looked for an alternative to silence them. The plan was to form a grass-roots organization with different goals. Emmanuel Constant, a former CIA informant, created the Front for the Advancement and Progress of Haiti, or FRAPH, which was made up of anti-Aristide paramilitary attachés. Their primary goal was to silence Aristide supporters with money, food or death if necessary. Constant was the son of Gerard Constant, a notorious member of the Tonton Macoutes. FRAPH thugs stormed and robbed homes at night. They forced fathers to have sex with their daughters and mothers to have sex with their sons. Sometimes they made the men watch while they raped their wives and daughters. Constant ordered gunmen to deliberately leave bodies lying in the streets as a silent message to anyone seeking democracy.

The hardship forced some partisans of Lavalas, the grass-roots pro-Aristide group, to defect to FRAPH for food and money. But the terror didn't prevent the people from protesting against a military that had no morals, no common sense. The leaders' greed for money and power had no limits. The masses were worn out, but they kept fighting to break the chains of injustice.

Thousands continued to flee Haiti in unsafe boats, only to be stopped by U.S. Coast Guard vessels or, worse, die trying. Aristide, who waited patiently to reclaim power, added fire to his words after months of silence by criticizing President Bill Clinton's Haiti policy, calling it racist.

I, too, thought it ironic that during his campaign for president, Clinton criticized his opponent, President Bush, for surrounding Haiti with Coast Guard ships that repatriated Haitians fleeing in boats. When he was elected, Clinton continued the policy, saying it was necessary to prevent Haitians from risking their lives in rickety boats. I wondered how Clinton,

a capitalist president, could care enough about Haitian lives. He promised Aristide that he would help restore the popular priest to power. Aristide believed Clinton at first, and appealed to his followers not to leave the impoverished island because he would return soon.

It appeared that Clinton was unwilling to tighten the arms and oil embargo and pressure Haitian military thugs to relinquish power, for U.S. officials weren't truly interested in supporting democracy in Haiti. Despite what the United States thought about Aristide, he was elected by nearly 67 percent of voters. Meanwhile, the Central Inteligence Agency attempted to assassinate Aristide's character, labeling him unstable.

It was a wave of violence that killed some prominent Haitians and forced the world to get involved. I watched in horror as television accounts showed edited clips of the assassination of Guy Malary, a wealthy lawyer who was gunned down on a Port-au-Prince street.

Aristide appointed Malary minister of justice after the Governors Island accord, which was signed in New York by Cedras and Aristide. I was in New York harbor as a photojournalist when they signed the deal in the summer of 1993. The agreement called for Cedras and other military leaders to resign. Port-au-Prince Police Chief Michel Francois, who took basic infantry training at Fort Benning, Ga., in 1981, was to resign as well. It also would have allowed Aristide to return as president on Oct. 30 of that year. (Robert Malval had been sworn in as prime minister in August that year. He resigned four months later, but remained acting prime minister for 11 more months.)

Aristide reluctantly signed the Governors Island accord because he said the Haitian leaders would not live up to it. He was right; Cedras signed the agreement so the embargo would be lifted while the leaders stockpiled weapons and ammunition.

As a member of a commission that drafted a law creating a new police force, Malary was seen as a direct threat to the power of Police Chief Francois. He was also heading the investigation of the murder a month earlier of Aristide supporter Antoine Izmery, who had organized a church service in memory of the victims of an attack that destroyed Aristide's parish church. Armed men stormed the church, dragged Izmery out, forced him to his knees and shot him in the head. The next year, the same paramilitary attachés murdered Father Jean-Marie Vincent, Aristide's close friend.

Aristide began to fight back. He embarked on a speaking circuit that took him from California to Boston, seeking support for his return to power. Haitians also turned up the heat. I was at the White House on special assignment when Clinton met Aristide in May 1994. The meeting drew an estimated 10,000 of Aristide's countrymen from around the nation. The speakers, some draped in the red and blue colors of the Haitian flag, protested in front of the White House. They urged Clinton to help restore Aristide to power. They also denounced the return of political refugees.

At many of the places where Aristide spoke in the United States, I traveled to that city to hear him speak. I was in Boston where he spoke to a crowd of mostly Haitians. "Our rights are violated when they send back our political refugees," he said. "Today's enemies of democracy keep Haitians on one side and the army on the other side to continue the genocide." He also called the oil and arms embargo, which was being ignored by Haiti's neighbor, the Dominican Republic, a sham. "It's a leaking embargo," he told listeners. "We didn't ask for this embargo imposed to break the struggle of Haitians fighting for democracy."

Aristide's outspokenness caught the attention of several members of the U.S. Congress. Six congressional members were arrested after they staged a sit-in in front of the White House. Other politicians called for a stronger U.S. stance. During a hearing on aid to Latin America, Democratic Rep. David R. Obey of Wisconsin, the House Appropriations Committee chairman at the time, said the United States should invade Haiti and arrest and jail its military leaders. "Haitians are being ground up like hamburger because the clowns who run that government don't know how to behave like adults," he said.

Prominent African Americans also put the pressure on the Clinton administration. Randall Robinson, head of TransAfrica, a foreign policy lobbying group, went on a hunger strike in protest of U.S. policy toward Haiti. Robinson also released a statement signed by 43 African Americans, including members of the

Congressional Black Caucus, calling for sanctions on oil and weapons imports to be expanded. The Rev. Jesse Jackson described the continuing dictatorship of Haiti as a massive case of "black-on-black crime," and suggested using military force as a last resort to restore democracy on the tiny island.

Although the United States never ruled out using military intervention, in the eyes of the international community it looked impotent when a band of thugs, paid by the military, brandished guns and refused to let the USS Harlan County dock in Haiti. The ship contained an international crew of 218 military advisers who were being sent to help train the Haitian military and separate it from the police force. This was part of the deal brokered for Aristide and Cedras.

As the pressure mounted, the Clinton administration made revisions in its Haitian policy. I applauded when Lawrence Pezzullo, the State Department's special envoy to Haiti, was removed. He had close ties with the Haitian military and had urged Aristide to work with political opponents in Haiti. The U.S. administration also pressed the United Nations to broaden the embargo that was imposed after the coup, so it covered all trade except food and medicine, and increased pressure on Haitian military leaders to step down.

"We don't ask for food, we ask for justice," Aristide said while speaking in Boston. "Once we have justice, we will feed ourselves."

One thing the president forgot was that justice didn't exist because the justice system in Haiti had been out of service for a long time. It could not be repaired overnight.

Although Haitian leaders showed no signs of stepping down before Aristide's return, I, along with other journalists from around the world, swarmed to Haiti to report on the event just in case. The atmosphere was tense. We were told to return to the hotel before dark because of violence. Gunshots rang out all night. The "zenglendo" waited until dark to break into peoples' houses to rob them.

One night, Franki and I were visiting a friend and we were late getting back to the hotel in Petionville. It was dark and rainy. While driving down one street, we encountered a roadblock. I got out of the car and threw the obstruction to the side. Armed men in the shadows eyed us but didn't say a word. Franki was afraid and called for me to hurry back to the car.

Further down the road, there was another roadblock. I saw an opening that I could drive through but a car had blocked the opening. The driver was talking to someone on the sidewalk. I blew my horn, and signaled with my hand for the driver to move along, but the car didn't budge. I blew the horn again. The driver angrily drove up close to my car and rolled down his car window. I rolled down my window, too. We sat there in the middle of the street staring at each other. Franki begged me to drive away. I was scared to death. But I kept staring at the man's angry face. He quickly sped off. I didn't explain it to Franki at the time, but in Haiti, if you show signs of weakness you can be killed. Because I stood my ground, the man assumed — wrongly — I was an attaché or zenglendo.

A few days later, I went with some other photojournalists to take pictures of an anti-Aristide protest at FRAPH headquarters near the Palace. A FRAPH member looked me in the eyes and said, "If any Haitian takes my picture, I will kill him right now." I pretended like I didn't speak Creole. I even wore a cap that I turned around backwards on my head. I took some pictures and quietly moved away from him. I was an easy target for gunmen who would kill a Haitian quicker than an American or other foreigner. They claim that the Haitian press is pro-Aristide.

I was glad to leave Haiti. Whenever I visit, I never know if I will return alive.

The embargo was finally tightened in late 1993 to punish Cedras for refusing to resign under the terms of the Governors Island agreement. Deep down, I felt Cedras would not keep his end of the bargain to step down and allow Aristide's return by the end of October 1993. I wasn't surprised when Cedras and the other military leaders who initiated the coup d'état reneged, because you can't tell a pig not to lie in the mud unless you keep it on a leash.

Aristide remained an exile in Washington until October 1994, when the U.S.-led embargo would become a U.S.-led invasion. ▶

Haitians sold
like beasts to plantation owners
who plopped them in slave quarters.

Slave masters
packed them like processed sugar
in steaming hot rooms that make their skin
glistens like crystal.

Modern day slaves
forced to work in sugar cane fields
from sunup to sundown without food,
their skin loose on their bones.

Haitians wear
misery on their face
like the old clothes
that hang loosely on their bodies.

ACROSS THE BORDER

My mother always told me no matter how hard it was to survive in Haiti, to never, never cross the border to seek a better life in the Dominican Republic. She was afraid I would be killed like the 30,000 Haitian workers that the late Dominican Republic President Rafael Leonidas Trujillo senselessly ordered his troops to massacre in 1937.

"It's better to be a living dog than a dead lion," my mother would often say.

But Aristide, while president, went a bit farther when he said, "Never again, never again will our Haitian sisters and brothers be sold to convert their blood into bitter sugar." He also demanded reparations for Haitians living in the Dominican Republic. Before he left office, Aristide met with former Dominican Republic President Joaquin Balaguer. I don't think anything concrete materialized.

Despite my mother's warning, 20 years later I did cross the border. I went not to work on a plantation like thousands of my countrymen still do, but as someone who cares about the plight of Haitians who live in Dominican bateys, and harvest sugar cane. Bateys range from small to large close-knit communities with run-down housing for field workers. Even though my mother never set foot in the Dominican Republic, she was right to advise me not to walk in the dangerous fields of sugar cane in that country.

When Aristide was in power, some of the Tonton Macoutes fled into hiding in the neighboring Dominican Republic, which shares the island of Hispaniola with Haiti. After the coup d'état in Haiti in 1991, pro-Aristide Haitians living in the Dominican Republic were also afraid because some coup leaders and Tonton Macoutes were there waiting to invade Haiti. After the United States imported democracy to Haiti, there was talk that the

Haitian government would also seek democratic and human rights for the thousands of Haitians who work in Dominican sugar-cane fields.

A few days after Franki and I witnessed Haiti's presidential election in December 1995, we visited the Dominican Republic. We wanted to see for ourselves if the horror stories we heard about Haitian slaves were true. We also wanted to see if Haitian and Dominican officials were really trying to work together to improve working and living conditions for Haitians.

We met with Guy Alexandre, the Haitian ambassador to the Dominican Republic. He told us that selling Haitians to the country was once an institution. But, he said, the contract ended when Duvalier left power in 1986. It was not until Haiti tried to become a democracy that people began calling the practice an abuse of human rights.

"Before 1986, no one talked about bateys," Alexandre said at the ambassador's residence in Santo Domingo, the capital city. "It's become an issue now and the government has been talking about it for a long time.

"The batey is inhuman," he continued. "The two governments have to sit down with a mediator. It's a problem that can't be solved overnight."

But while visiting several bateys, we found that nothing had been done to help the workers and their families. In fact, we found the conditions similar to former slave plantations in the United States' Deep South. We met several workers like Eric St.

Vil who lived in a one-room shack. We spent a day with him and his family.

Each morning St. Vil, 31, gets up early and straps his machete around his small waist. He and another cane cutter walk several miles to the hot, dusty sugar-cane fields. That day we were there, he wore a thick, long-sleeve shirt and pants, and boots for protection from the towering plants. We went to the sugar-cane field where the lanky St. Vil works 12 hours or more.

He is just one of the 500,000 Haitians who left their country to work as braceros, or cane cutters, in the Dominican Republic. Because Dominicans consider cutting cane demeaning work, the government sends recruiters, known as buscones, to Haiti to solicit their neighbors to do the backbreaking work. They promise recruits good pay and decent housing.

Upon their arrival, Haitians face a form of enslavement on the plantations. New arrivals, called kongos, are prohibited from wandering too far from the plantations because their owners fear they will flee. They are imprisoned in the bateys. There are between 250 and 500 bateys in the Dominican Republic, yet the Dominican government refuses to give the Haitians who live in them legal resident status, no matter how long they have lived in the country. Even children born to Haitian parents are not recognized as citizens. They are considered people in transition.

The State Sugar Council, or CEA, runs most of the country's plantations and operates some of the unions, which are disorganized and have no power. Human-rights violations are rampant. A group of Haitian and Haitian-Dominican women have banded together to fight, especially for the rights of women in the bateys who suffer the brunt of the abuses. Women lack education, employment rights and health care. If a woman's husband abandons her, she has to leave the batey because only families of field hands are allowed to stay. Eventually, she is raped or forced into prostitution to support herself and her children.

Despite the deplorable conditions, Haitians leave their poor country in search of what they hope is a better life across the border.

Haitians have been coming to the Dominican Republic since the early 1900s. They began arriving during the fall sugar-cane season after America invaded Haiti in 1915 and then occupied the Spanish-speaking country from 1916 to 1924. Foreigners began to buy land and harvest sugar cane, and Haitians were brought in as cheap labor to cut it.

Migrant workers faced resentment from their Spanish-speaking neighbors, who never forgave Haitians for occupying their country in 1822. It was when sugar demand decreased during the U.S. Depression that President Trujillo ordered the massacre of 30,000 Haitians. After an international investigation, Trujillo paid the Haitian government $750,000 for the loss.

But in the mid-1960s, the corrupt and greedy Francois "Papa Doc" Duvalier established an agreement as Haitian president with the Dominican government to trade Haitian peasants as field hands. Papa Doc sold 20,000 Haitians to the Dominicans

for roughly $2 million. The contract expired after his son, Jean-Claude "Baby Doc" Duvalier, fled the country in 1986.

"Duvalier sold us and we couldn't go back; we would've been killed," said Henri George Janvier, 53, a part-time cane cutter who also owns a store at Batey Tabacones. "We are treated like slaves." He recalled how a man refused to go to the fields one day, and the foreman took the man's machete, beat him with it, and forced him to work.

Janvier left Haiti and went to the Dominican Republic at age 20. He has a wife and three young children. Standing behind the counter in the small store attached to his house, he said many Haitians don't like living in the country but, "Haiti is not better because there're no jobs."

Janvier said cane cutters don't know how much money they earn. He explained that each cutter is allotted a certain area to harvest in the sprawling green fields. They cut the cane to fill a large container, which is taken to the factory and weighed by Dominican workers. This process can take days or weeks. If the cane is worth 70 pesos, the Dominicans may cheat you out of 40, he said.

St. Vil said cane cutters don't receive cash or checks for their labor. They get "trade receipts," which state who they work for and how much they earned. They use the meager vouchers to buy little more than food at the batey's small store.

St. Vil and his family of six live in a one-room row house with no plumbing or electricity. A water pump out back serves the whole batey. His common-law wife, Monique Jean, cooked outside in a smoky makeshift kitchen made of sticks and rags and a thatch roof. The stove consisted of a pile of three rocks and wood elevated on a wooden stand.

Inside their home, a piece of cloth divided the room in half. Behind the partition was a cot and bundles of clothing in a corner. On the other side was a table, two chairs, and a battery-operated radio. Pots and pans hung on the wall.

The dusty batey where they live is a small community of close-knit families. The nearest town and paved road to the batey is about 20 miles away. Bumpy dirt roads lead to the isolated area, surrounded by never-ending rows of sweet, juicy sugar cane that surround the batey like a wall.

The men work in the fields all day and the women cook, clean and take care of the children. They played with each other or sat around the batey with the adults, who wore misery on their faces like the old clothes that hung loosely on their thin bodies. None of the children attended school.

Most of the older people still speak their native Creole, and Spanish. The majority of the young children who were born in the Dominican Republic only speak Spanish. Although the government doesn't recognize them as citizens, the children say they are Dominican.

"The only thing to do around here is cut sugar cane," St. Vil said. "There's no future here. My children can't go to school." He said the schools are far away and he has no transportation.

Besides, schools cost money, which he doesn't have.

Jean said she washed clothes for other people, but the money was not enough to make ends meet. She and her parents left Haiti when she was a small girl. She doesn't know how old she is, but St. Vil suspects she's in her early 30s. Jean already had two children when she met St. Vil, who planned to return to Haiti after he made a bundle of money.

Reality set in when they discovered that kongos can't freely leave the plantation. Men on horses, the major-domo, constantly patrol the area. Even if cane cutters were free to leave the Dominican Republic, they can't earn enough money to pay their fare back to Haiti. They need a visa to cross the border, which cost 35 U.S. dollars when we were there. The six-and-a-half hour bus fare to Port-au-Prince costs 35 U.S. dollars.

Jose Guillermo Beltre Rogiers, a Dominican who supervises roughly 500 workers in five bateys, said new field hands aren't allowed to come and go as they please because government officials pay for their transportation here and they don't want the workers to leave and work for another company.

The Haitian plight, however, hasn't gone unnoticed.

Sonia Pierre, who was born in a batey, is now an advocate for women. She was among the immigrant delegation from Santo Domingo who went to the International Women's Conference a few years ago in China. Pierre is coordinator of social, legal and human rights for Movimento de Mujeres Dominico Haitiana Inc., or MUDHA, a private organization supporting the rights of

Haitian and Haitian-Dominican women.

"The government doesn't recognize us as being a part of society," Pierre said. "They consider women 'braceros' makers who produce more children who will grow up to be cane cutters."

Pierre remembers the problems that women in the batey endure. She saw girls as young as 12 moving in with old men because their parents could no longer care for them. She said if a woman has children and no husband, but wants to remain in the batey, she must provide sexual favors for the major-domo or batey supervisor. Still, Pierre adds, he may force her to leave after he loses interest.

Pierre said about 60 percent of the women are heads of households, including her mother, who worked day and night planting and cutting cane to feed her 12 children. After 43 years, her mother still lives in the batey with no benefits or health insurance. If one of her sons didn't work in the fields, she would be forced to move.

Pierre is not alone in the struggle for Haitians' human rights. Edwin Paraison, 35, a Haitian consul in Barahona, Dominican Republic, has been an advocate for Haitians for more than a decade. He oversees four provinces with 22 bateys under his jurisdiction. Before Aristide's government appointed him consular, Paraison had lived in the Dominican Republic since 1983 working with Haitians. The Episcopal Church began an outreach program for Haitian workers living in the country and brought some priests from Haiti to train.

Paraison's primary goal was to organize Haitians and promote and defend their human rights. He said he used to protest in the streets, but now his tactics have changed. "I've made things good and bad," he said, referring to his late 1994 appointment. "Now that I've become a consul, there are some things I can't do. I have rules to abide by."

He still acts as an advocate for Haitians who are jailed, hospitalized or beaten. While an Episcopal priest, Paraison was kicked out of the church for spreading the word internationally about the treatment of Haitians living in the Dominican Republic. A London-based anti-slavery group honored his work with Haitians and invited him to speak about the situation during a 10-day trip to London.

The bishop told him not to go. When Paraison returned, the bishop said he was insubordinate and gave him 10 days to leave the church.

He had about 40 U.S. dollars in the bank, no job and nowhere to go. He lived with another priest while looking for another church. When Aristide, a former priest, was restored to power, he offered Paraison the consulate job, because he had heard about his work with Haitians living in the Dominican Republic.

Paraison, who began working for the Haitian government in February 1995, says the Dominican government refuses to recognize him as a Haitian official. He can't even issue visas. He believes the Dominican government considers him a traitor who tried to destroy business and tourism in the country.

But Paraison said his only crime was trying to uphold Haitians' civil rights, such as illegal deportations. Dominican military officers frequently arrest Haitian men walking down the street, he said, and drop them off at the border, without notifying Haitian authorities. The men aren't allowed to go home, pack, collect their wages, or say goodbye to their families.

Four years ago, he said, the Dominican government recognized there was a Haitian problem. In a strong show to the international community, he said, officials signed a decree to improve working conditions and grant the foreign workers human rights. Shortly after the signing, 5,000 Haitians were sent back to Haiti without explanation.

So far, nothing has changed. Maybe things will be better for the Haitians at the bateys in the Dominican Republic when Aristide becomes president in 2001. ◗

Oh democracy!
I heard about you
ever since I was born,
but I never experienced you.

Oh democracy!
My heart laments for you
all day, all night.

Oh democracy!
Don't run away from me
help me to stop . . .
the bloodshed.

Oh democracy!
remember all those
people who were killed
just for
seeking . . . you
but the one
made in America.

OPERATION UPHOLD DEMOCRACY

My mother was born during the first U.S. occupation of Haiti. She was 15 years old when the Marines left the country in 1934, but she was old enough to understand what her mother told her about the invasion, and see what the U.S. Marines did to Haiti. She called the events that unfolded the "rape of my country." She said they raped the women, raped the peasants, raped the economy, and raped the constitution.

"I hope I never see those Yankee boots again," she said, her voice choking.

She had died when the American eagle landed in Haiti once again, on Sept. 19, 1994. They were there to restore democracy, sent by President Bill Clinton to a country where its leaders ruled for almost 200 years with repression and brutality.

I knew my mother would have had a heart attack if she had seen U.S. helicopters hovering in Haiti's skies like a group of predatory birds. The sight of U.S. soldiers jumping from the camouflaged helicopters would have frightened her to death. The Marines lay flat on the ground, their loaded automatic weapons cocked to fire on their enemy. Their heavy knapsacks were full of democracy imported from America. The cowardly Haitian soldiers offered no resistance as the U.S. force quickly swelled to 20,000 troops, in addition to 300 soldiers from the Caribbean community.

Raoul Cedras, Haiti's de facto leader who helped lead the coup that overthrew Aristide, tried to use former President Jimmy Carter to head off the invasion. Clinton, in a television address to the United States, said an invasion was inevitable unless Cedras resigned. I remember how my blood surged when Clinton said he had the right as commander in chief to send troops into Haiti to restore its legitimate, constitutional government. But my feelings were in conflict. On the one hand, I wanted Aristide returned, but I was against an invasion because of what happened in 1915, when the United States entered Haiti to put a stop to its political bloodshed. Haiti experienced numerous periods of intense political and economic disorder, having 22 changes of government from 1843 until 1915, when the Marines invaded. The United States withdrew in 1934 at the request of the elected government of Haiti. The U.S. soldiers believed Haitians had the mindset of children and treated them badly. Haitians were determined to prevent this from happening again.

Shortly after Clinton's speech, former President Carter, U.S. Sen. Sam Nunn and ex-General Colin Powell left for Haiti on Sept. 16, 1994, to negotiate with the military junta. Carter's team cut a sweet deal with Cedras. I knew Carter and his team did not represent the masses, and the people used graffiti to express their opposition and outrage. "Aba Carter" (Down with Carter) and "Carter se atache" (Carter is a thug) were scribbled on walls everywhere in Port-au-Prince.

Carter seemed hesitant when he said he didn't know who was responsible for the atrocities in Haiti, because the society's violent divisions were extreme. He should have asked the CIA who had ties with Haiti military officials whose reign of terror included executions and rape. But after the coup plotters went into exile with their bloody hands, the people saw their nightmare disappear like smoke in the cloudy sky.

I arrived in Haiti a few days after the Marines landed, and talked to some of my countrymen about the two invasions. Their feelings were mixed.

Marcell Assad, 95 at the time, was against the second American invasion. He was 13 at the time of the first invasion, and was able to recall in detail when, in July 1915, a hungry mob dragged the tyrannical president Vilbrun Guillaume Sam from a closet in the French Embassy where he took refuge. They tore him to pieces because he had ordered 300 prisoners killed.

Within a week, on July 28, 1915, Assad said he and his friends saw a U.S. ship fueled by coal and darkened by smoke, anchored offshore in Port-au-Prince. "I thought a boat was on fire," he recalled. "My father said, 'Oh my God, the U.S. Marines invaded Haiti.' We were afraid because we thought the Marines were going to kill us." The Marines were welcomed by the indigent Haitian army and the bourgeois. The countryside was affected the most during the 1915 occupation. More than 5,000 peasants were killed in Marchaterre by Marines during a peaceful march to protest the harsh conditions.

Assad said the difference between the first invasion in 1915 and the second one was that the latter one was misunderstood. "In 1915, it was a physical occupation," Assad said. "The peasants were humiliated and forced to work from 10 to 15 hours daily. If they refused, U.S. Marines and rural sheriffs beat them." Assad said the 1994 invasion was psychological. Why 20,000 troops? he said the Haitian people asked. Why the big ships in Haiti's waters? Why all the aircraft in a small country like Haiti? They were puzzled, he said, by the numerous helicopters, bulldozers, tractors, and armed soldiers everywhere.

The Marines built new roads and repaired existing ones throughout Haiti, with forced labor to benefit U.S. companies. I wonder how Aristide felt while receiving a 21-gun salute at the Pentagon during a demagogic ceremony. Aristide betrayed Charlemagne Peralte. He betrayed Jean-Jacques Dessalines, one of the Haitian leaders who fought the French for Haiti's independence.

The United States claimed that the purpose of the first occupation was to better the lives of Haitians and to end the tyranny, bestialization, and oppression that existed in Haiti. But the United States took over our country and carried out reforms for its own interests. I felt the occupation was humiliating because Haitians were forced to betray Charlemagne Peralte. It was also a sad day for our nation because our ancestors had fought and died for our independence.

My uncle Aldoff Verna, who passed away recently at 79, was the griot of the family. He said the most humiliating thing that happened to Haiti was when Franklin D. Roosevelt, then assistant secretary of the Navy, rewrote the Haitian constitution to make foreigners eligible to own real estate for the first time in Haiti. U.S. investors acquired tens of thousands of acres of land from peasants who were expelled from their property and then forced to work on the same land they had owned. After this cruel act by the United States, the masses resented the occupation, especially peasants.

It was then, according to my uncle, that a group of peasants led by Charlmagne Peralte formed a peasant army called Cacos. Its mission was to defend peasants abused by the Marines and to overthrow the puppet president, Sudre Datiguenave. They were upset that Datiguenave gave Haitian financial institutions and customs to the United States. Peralte and members of his peasant army were killed in an ambush by the Marines, who acted with the blessing of the Haitian government. He became a symbol of resistance for Haitians. The remnants of the peasant army went underground and continued the struggle until 1934 when Roosevelt, as U.S. president, ended the occupation. My mother said that was the happiest day of her life.

In contrast to the 1915 occupation, thousands of poor Haitians welcomed the Marines on Sept. 19, 1994. They carried the troops on their shoulders and thanked them for coming to save the people from a brutal military. Ironically, the Haitian military was established by the United States a half-century ago to protect U.S. interests at the end of the first occupation.

The troops were part of a peacekeeping force sent to prepare the country for Aristide's restoration to power. They were also there to make sure the Haitian generals stepped down before Aristide's return. Of course, Aristide returned to defend the interests of the U.S. government, much like former Sudre Dartiguenave did as president during the first occupation.

I looked beyond what U.S. officials said and focused on their deeds. Historically, the U.S. government has kept close ties with the Haitian military, training and grooming its dictators for the United States' own interests. Many Haitian political leaders have been on the payroll of the CIA, including Raoul Cedras and Police Chief Michel Francois. Also on the CIA's payroll at one time — before he was dismissed — was Emmanuel Constant, the leader of FRAPH.

Because of the United States' relationship with Haiti's military leaders, I knew it was a joke when I heard and read news reports that the multinational peacekeeping force seized and destroyed the Haitian military's heavy weapons, and broken up FRAPH. The Marines also set up a weapons buyback program, in which people would turn in their guns for cash. During the 1915 occupation, the Marines bought back weapons too.

"I would like to know where all the M-16s, machine guns, and hand grenades came from?" my uncle Aldoff angrily asked while watching the news on CNN during a visit at his son's home in New York.

In reality, the thugs turned in only old weapons that no longer worked. Anti-Aristide groups were still heavily armed and patiently waiting for the foreign troops to leave the country.

I soon realized that the U.S. occupation of Haiti had nothing to do with democracy, because democracy cannot be imported.

The United States tried to convince the world that democracy had been reinstated in Haiti. After weeks of being spectators, U.S. troops raided FRAPH headquarters in broad daylight — a well-prepared scenario. The plan was not to protect the people against armed paramilitary attachés, but to seize classified documents before the people looted the place.

No one knows how and when Emmanuel Constant came to the United States. U.S. officials later arrested him for using an expired visa to enter the country. I suspect that the United States flew in Constant because it is virtually impossible to get into this country without proper legal papers. Customs are tight at Haiti's airport because the United States will fine an airline that allows a passenger to board its aircraft illegally. In addition, U.S. Customs agents closely inspect passports and visas upon arrival.

For months, the U.S. threatened to deport Constant back to Haiti so he could be tried for crimes he committed while Aristide was in exile. However, after Constant, the former CIA informant, threatened to talk about the agency's involvement with crimes in Haiti, he was suddenly released from jail. I wasn't surprised about the CIA's involvement in the crimes that happened in Haiti during the coup d'état.

In Haiti, the U.S. soldiers put on a show to regain the confidence of Haitians who questioned if they were there to protect democracy. I saw Marines handcuff low-ranked Haitian soldiers and push them to the ground in front of the National Palace. They arrested soldiers for human rights violations while Marine Maj. Gen. John Sheehan had a good time with Lieutenant General Cedras at a reception.

Meanwhile, the political, social and economic structure in

Haiti began to die. Popular and grass-roots organizations were destabilized. Aristide had more than a year left in power. What could he accomplish that would satisfy the population? The World Bank and International Monetary Fund promised Aristide that upon his return, they would lend his country millions of dollars to help it on its feet. In addition, USAID, a key player in Haiti, offered millions in assistance. But it was only a promise because the country waited, waited and waited, like a beggar at the gate of the United States.

I figured that foreign troops were there to protect military leaders and the rich, for poor Haitians were still being killed and abused by the authorities, all in the name of democracy. There was no military presence in poor neighborhoods. Most of the soldiers were stationed in the hills where the wealthy lived and around downtown businesses. I wasn't surprised when the U.S. Army court-martialed Captain Lawrence P. Rockwood, of the 10th Mountain Division, for conducting an unauthorized inspection at the Penitentiary National in Port-au-Prince, where Aristide supporters had been kept in a 50-by-40 foot cell. This was a human-rights violation perpetrated by the multinational forces in Haiti.

My wife, Franki, and I went to talk to some of the troops who lived in the sprawling tents near the Port-au-Prince airport. Some were confused about their duty in Haiti. A few said they didn't know why they were there. Others were pleased with the fat paychecks they received for their tour of duty.

Some, however, said they felt good about the humanitarian mission.

Sgt. Alejandro Nieto was with the 10th Mountain Division, based at Fort Drum, N.Y.

"If it's going to make a difference, I'm all for it," said Nieto, the father of three sons. "The kids stand at the fence saying they're glad we're here. It makes us feel like we're doing something."

Nieto said the warm welcome helped him cope on the Caribbean island. "It's not bad, it could've been worse," he said. "'There's no one shooting at us, like in Somalia."

The Marines weren't allowed to go outside their location for recreation. When they did go out for business in the sweltering heat, they had to wear full gear, including helmet, boots and bulletproof vests. To relieve some of the stress, they were gradually given some time for rest and relaxation at a hotel in the countryside for a few days.

"This place is like a vacation compared to Somalia," said Sgt. Michael Smith, 20, who worked eight-hour shifts in communications, setting up radio transmissions with other units. "Somalia had a higher threat level; the compound in Somalia had a lot more guard duty."

Although he described Haitians as nice people, he didn't understand why U.S. troops had to be there. "We came here for no reason; there's no threat," he said. "We're a support unit doing humanitarian work. That's about it."

Sgt. Rodney Harris, 26, said he liked doing humanitarian support and that most soldiers had a "real positive attitude" about it. But, he added, a lot of new soldiers who were right out of high school and have never been abroad were frightened. "I was more scared and on my toes in Somalia," he said. "There were snipers and people shooting. It's more relaxed over here."

Some Haitians believed that regardless of the United States' humanitarian effort, the Americans were trying to displace the French, who still have strong ties to Haiti, which won its independence in 1804.

In poor neighborhoods, "Americans for 50 Years" was scribbled on walls everywhere. But the jubilation ended abruptly when poor Haitians realized the troops were not there to protect them. They were there to protect Lieutenant General Raoul Cedras, a CIA informer, as he and his officers prepared to go into exile. ◗

VIII

Give democracy a chance
chanted the crowd
while General Iron Fist
passed the bloody torch
to General Puppet.

Give us back our country
now, blood-shedder . . .
sang the masses while running
after ex-general's convoy
on its way to a golden
exile in Panama.

IRON FIST GENERAL

My mother would have lighted a candle on Oct. 10, 1994, in front of army headquarters in memory of her brother, who was killed by military thugs at Fort Dimanche prison. I wanted to be in Haiti on that sad day to witness the downfall of the Haitian military that made us weep day and night. Unfortunately, I wasn't able to get a flight home. I was perturbed as I watched the demagogic ceremony on television orchestrated by the Marines for the last of the iron fists, Lieutenant General Raoul Cedras. I wanted to cry criminal, you can't leave the country with the blood of my brother, the blood of my uncles and the blood of all innocent people on your hands, but I was frozen and voiceless. It occurred early on a Monday. The morning clouds seemed to cry with thousands of Haitians as they sang traditional funeral songs to Cedras in front of military headquarters.

Cedras, his predecessors General Prosper Avril and Lieutenant General Henri Namphy, ruled the country during the last decade. They killed innocent people, robbed the country's coffers and left Haiti under the protection of the U.S. military. This time the iron fist general and his associates went free with the blessing of Aristide's government and the sordid Parliament. In spite of accusations of corruption and bloodshed, the popular regime agreed to give amnesty to these military thugs. It was a setback for the country because the victims and their families expected the government to create a popular tribunal for judging the criminals. Regrettably, money and power were more important for the Lavalas leadership than justice.

Cedras and Brigadier General Philippe Biamby, the army's chief of staff, agreed to resign when they learned that American paratroopers were on their way in a scheduled Sunday night raid. The attack would not have been postponed if the dictators had not agreed to resign. Former U.S. President Jimmy Carter had visited at midday the day before, and it was then that he warned Haitian officials that an invasion was imminent, within hours, even minutes, unless the leaders resigned and accepted the return of Aristide.

Under the arrangement, Cedras and Biamby agreed to step down from power by Oct. 15, 1994, or after Parliament passed an amnesty law. Michel Francois, the powerful Port-au-Prince police chief, also stepped down. Cedras demanded a blanket pardon for him and the rest of the army for crimes committed during the 1991 coup and the repressive dictatorship that followed it. The agreement, however, didn't require the generals to leave Haiti.

I was appalled at the free ride given to Cedras, Biamby and Francois. What about the atrocities they took part in during the three years of Aristide's exile? Did Clinton forget his threat that they resign immediately or be forced out by U.S. troops?

In addition to the amnesty law, the economic embargo and financial, visa and travel sanctions were also lifted. This was good news for Franki and me, for we had been trying to get a flight to Haiti to witness Aristide's historic return. Because of the embargo, all commercial airlines had stopped flying to Haiti.

Aristide is the only exiled Haitian president who ever regained power. In hindsight, I'm sure Cedras and his military junta are deeply sorry they didn't kill Aristide the night of the coup d'état. They probably never envisioned Aristide returning to Haiti.

Many Haitians missed work and school to attend Cedras' farewell ceremony. When he delivered his farewell speech, thousands of Haitians sang "Auld Lang Syne" in Creole and jeered him. Some crowed like roosters, which is the symbol of Aristide's political party. The loud noise made it hard to hear Cedras' speech and the playing of the Haitian national anthem.

The people waved U.S. flags and pictures of Aristide, while Cedras passed the torch of blood to puppet Brigadier General Jean Claude Duperval. The new general also became a puppet in the hands of the U.S military.

After Cedras left the country, the 7,000-man Haitian army was in trouble. Cedras' departure closed a long chapter of military presence in Haiti. The army had directly or indirectly controlled the country economically, politically and socially. Almost half of the national budget went to the military, which symbolized repression, death, devastation, dictatorship and destruction. All of this supposedly collapsed with Cedras' exit.

Ever since Haiti's independence, the army divided the country into clans and classes of power and wealth. Until 1957, when Francois "Papa Doc" Duvalier became president, about 34 of the country's 36 heads of state were overthrown in coup d'états. This is probably why Aristide eventually abolished the military, which incarcerated people at the feared Fort Dimanche military barracks.

My uncle Nicolas Remy, a survivor of Fort Dimanche, said the Tonton Macoutes took him there in a car. He said the car moved slowly, so slow it seemed like he was following his own funeral procession. The Macoutes forced him face down on the floor of the car while they inflicted on him all kinds of unspeakable abuses. The outlaws thought my uncle was already dead, because only God could spare your life at Fort Dimanche. My uncle recalled that when he arrived at Fort Dimanche, the Macoutes showed him what would happen to a political prisoner — he would be killed point blank.

He awaited what he believed would be his execution incarcerated in a small cell under bright light bulbs of up to 400 watts. He said it was so hot that after a few minutes he was soaked from head to toe. The hell-like cell was built especially for "communists" who conspired to overthrow Papa Doc.

In 1994, after the U.S. invasion and occupation, the Haitian army feared retribution from a mob that gathered at the now-abandoned prison. It was a good time for me to visit the cemetery where many innocent people were killed and buried in unmarked graves. My other uncle, Mirabeau Alexandre, was among those killed. The concentration camp was located in the middle of nowhere; even in broad daylight I was afraid to walk in the 5-foot tall grass to get there. As I approached the defaced building, it looked like an old grave. I stood in front of the bright yellow prison for a moment in silence. I remembered my uncle before I walked into the dilapidated prison.

The grimy walls inside were stained with blood in every room. I could hear the voice of my uncle screaming for help while his torturers pulled out his fingernails one by one, before they murdered him. At the time, I couldn't find words to express my feelings about Fort Dimanche. So I later wrote a poem. ▶

Fort Dimanche,
a human butcher shop
owned and operated by torturers
licensed to commit atrocities.

Fort Dimanche,
a final walk in a cemetery
for the powerless.

Fort Dimanche.
Inside, a lake of blood,
a forest of human bones.

Fort Dimanche,
a monument of shame
in the hearts of all Haitians.

Fort Dimanche,
a fort for martyrs
who refused to be silent.

Fort Dimanche,
a grave for Haitians
assassinated without cause.

Fort Dimanche,
a memorial for the people
who died without
saying good-bye.

Fort Dimanche.
A prison of no return.

IX

Peace for which we suffer.
Peace for which we
gave our lives for is not peace.
It's just an illusion of peace.

THE MESSIAH OF THE POOR

If my mother had lived to see the triumphant return of the messiah of the poor, she would not have been happy to see Jean-Bertrand Aristide walk out of a U.S. Air Force plane. It would have brought back a lot of memories.

On Oct. 14, 1994, the day before the United States restored the messiah of the poor to power with a powerful show of military force, I rejoiced all night with celebrants. We went from neighborhood to neighborhood, reveling in the fever of democracy that we passed to each other. I hadn't seen that kind of jubilation since 1986 after Baby Doc fled the country.

But I was also afraid when we passed in front of FRAPH's headquarters, because I knew those outlaws could blow up all of us with a grenade. I was relieved when we left that location. The

people's faces expressed hope for the moment. But what would happen in the long run? We were so hungry for democracy we forgot that it was made in the United States, in collaboration with the international community.

Haitians organized vigils throughout the country, including one in front of the National Palace. After my democratic fever wore off, I thought about what the future would bring for my countrymen. While the masses continued to chant and dance in the streets, I questioned why President Clinton risked American lives for a small Caribbean country like Haiti?

After three years of convoluted negotiations, after three years of repression against impoverished Haitians, after three years of ineffective embargoes that helped the aggressors pile up fortunes, the majority of Haitians finally welcomed Aristide with open hearts.

When Aristide reclaimed power on Oct. 15, 1994, I wanted to know what his mission was for Haiti. Was he sent back to accomplish the international community's plan? Did he come back to work for the people who elected him president and fought for his return to power? Could Aristide satisfy both parties? Indeed, Clinton cautioned Aristide against any retaliation or extreme political acts. In turn, he promised Clinton that he would discourage his supporters from seeking revenge against the military or the wealthy elite who supported the coup. Some middle-class Haitians I spoke with said they considered former U.S. Ambassador William L. Swing president of Haiti because he was the one who made decisions for the country.

Meanwhile, the world watched as Aristide took his rightful seat as head of the country. I was at Port-au-Prince International Airport at 9 a.m., waiting for Aristide's return. The Hartford Courant, the newspaper in Connecticut I work for, sent me to cover the historical event. I was standing on the balcony among more than 100 journalists in the unrelenting sun. Security was tight. When I went to the bathroom, a U.S. soldier escorted me inside the airport and waited until I finished. He then escorted me back to the balcony. Finally, after hours of waiting, the plane landed. I felt my blood pulsating through my veins. When I saw President Aristide walk from the Boeing 707, one of the airplanes normally used by the U.S. secretary of state, I was surprised. I

wondered why Aristide chose such a plane. I thought he would come back on a chartered aircraft.

Later, at the National Palace, I found out from a pool of reporters that it was Aristide's decision to return in a U.S. military aircraft. During the flight back to Haiti, Aristide said there was no hiding the fact that he was brought back through U.S. intervention.

In addition to a U.S. delegation with Aristide, there were some Haitian officials, including then-Foreign Minister Claudette Werleigh; Rene Preval; Mildred Trouillot, an attorney who would later become Aristide's wife; Information Minister Herve Denis; and Central Bank Gov. Roger Perondin.

Aristide was visibly shaken and afraid when he stepped off the plane. He must have heard about the rumors that Haitian soldiers planned to assassinate him when he descended from the plane. Maybe that's why he asked for U.S. escorts. There was a lot of confusion that day at the airport, especially between U.S. Secret Service agents who accompanied Aristide and Haitian security officers. They looked like two groups of dummies who couldn't speak each other's language trying to communicate. The same thing happened at the National Palace.

After a short ceremony at the airport, Aristide walked under the gun of the U.S. military to a U.S. helicopter that flew him to the National Palace, where he hid behind a shield of bulletproof glass. He preached a new theology, a theology of reconciliation without justice that he learned from his capitalist teachers during his exile in Washington, D.C.

"Today is the day that the sun of democracy rises, never to set," Aristide said. "Today is the day that the eyes of justice open, never to close again. Today is the day that security takes over morning, noon and night."

Aristide had returned to a country that had suffered irreparable political turmoil. I wondered how he would overcome the hatred and suspicion and build Haiti into a democratic nation? Still, the people put their faith in Aristide. I talked to many who were willing to give him time to put his house in order. They understood the game the international community played with Aristide.

But Haitians were also frightened by Aristide's message of reconciliation. We wanted justice first —then reconciliation. We wanted the military and paramilitary criminals punished for the crimes they committed. We knew it would be difficult for Aristide to fulfill our dreams. But we were willing to wait patiently even if he made progress with turtle steps.

Aristide's only accomplishment was disbanding the military and creating a national police force, against the wishes of the United States. It was the only power he had during the 15 months left in his term. Within a month of his return, his nominee for prime minister, Smarck Michel, and a new cabinet were sworn in.

Meanwhile, the political, social and economic structure in Haiti began to die. Popular and grass-roots organizations waited for improvements. Aristide had little more than a year in power. What else could he accomplish that would satisfy the population?

The World Bank and International Monetary Fund promised Aristide that upon his return, they would lend Haiti millions of dollars to help the poor nation get back on its feet. USAID, a key player in Haiti, offered $555 million in assistance. But after Aristide took office, the promises and offers never materialized. The country still crawled in the mud to USAID offices like begging, homeless children. Some Haitians didn't care that they were hungry. They trusted Aristide to give them food and take care of them. They believed life would be better for them because he was back. They didn't know that Aristide returned as a figurehead, a puppet of the U.S. government.

The United States brought Aristide back a year before his term was over to calm the people, and to hold new presidential elections.

This was a new Aristide, not the same theologist who preached at St. Jean Bosco Catholic Church against the bourgeoisie and America. He had become a capitalist and a friend of the bourgeoisie. He had become a politician, and was no longer an activist. He had become someone who promised everything, even though he had nothing to give. After completing his training in Washington, he learned how to forget the peasants and deal with the bourgeois, for they had the money.

Haiti became like a museum during the first three months of Aristide's return to power. People came to look, to make deals and seek jobs. Aristide could not create jobs or distribute food, but he gave the people something more valuable — the destruction of the feared military. A military that was the source of the country's problems.

While in exile in Washington, Aristide got numerous offers from the international community, but once he returned to Haiti, the promises of aid never became reality. His hands were tied. He could do nothing for the people.

Did Aristide accomplish his dream? Did everyone sit down at the table as he promised during his campaign? Did he change the lives of all Haitian people? What legacy did he leave for the country? Has misery been wiped out because the messiah is back? Or, has the country fallen back into its corrupt ways like it has throughout history?

The poor still believed in Aristide, although the wheel of injustice turned brother against brother for a loaf of bread in the name of survival. This was a shame for a democratic country that couldn't feed its own people. The people waited while Aristide's so-called transparent government became opaque with corruption. If Aristide could have turned his promises into food, there would not be abnormally swollen bellies in Haiti. ❭

Yesterday,
you were a peasant.
Today,
you are a capitalist.
Yesterday,
you were a priest.
Today,
you are a husband.
Yesterday,
you were a liberator.
Today,
you are a vulture.

110

BOGUS HONEYMOON

My mother, who went to Mass every day, would have lost faith in the Catholic Church if she had lived to see her parish priest marry. In Haiti, 80 percent of the population is Catholic and the people believe priests are saints. To them, clergymen represent God and can do no wrong. I heard a lot of bad things about priests while growing up in Haiti, but I could never discuss such things with my mother. To her, a priest was a saint who saw God every day.

My mother would have been upset to see Aristide marry. I, too, was upset because I didn't get an invitation to the elaborate wedding. It apparently got lost in the mail with all the other invitations addressed to Aristide's mostly poor supporters in the ghettos of Port-au-Prince. Yet prominent Americans like Rep. Joseph Kennedy,

activist Randall Robinson and other dignitaries received theirs.

On Jan. 20, 1996, Jean-Bertrand Aristide, who had previously claimed he was married to the poor of Haiti, ended his honeymoon with them. He took another wife from the social class and country he denounced before becoming president. Aristide's political stronghold was in the slums of Haiti where he preached the theology of liberation, which took root in Latin America. The theme behind the theology is that the poor have a right to share in the world's prosperity.

But Aristide preached a different tune after returning from exile. Now was his time to enjoy the money he accumulated by only God knows how, and to start a family. It was reported that Aristide met Mildred Trouillot at a meeting with Haitian-

American lawyers in New York during his exile. After months of rumors about marriage, Aristide gave the country a first lady 17 days before he passed power to Preval. Aristide, the son of peasants from Port Salut, jumped a high broom to marry Trouillot, his former legal adviser, whom he paid a fat salary during his plush exile in Washington.

The fiery priest became popular during Jean-Claude Duvalier's reign as a frequent critic of the bourgeois and as a champion of the poor. He sought power in the name of the forgotten, the poor and the homeless. After becoming president, he followed suit of his predecessors by marrying the daughter of his oppressors. This was the practice of some Tonton Macoutes during the Duvalier era.

While Aristide was in exile, thousands of people seeking a better future for their families lost their lives by protesting in the streets against the iron-fisted regime that overthrew him. Aristide, who refused to compromise with the Vatican and give up politics, later relinquished his priesthood for his own selfish reasons, not in the interest of the people he supposedly represented.

About 500 guests were invited to Aristide's mansion, in the Port-au-Prince neighborhood of Tabarre, for the elaborate wedding. Many guests were world leaders who supported Aristide during his years in exile. None, however, were the poor, illiterate, hungry people who sacrificed their lives for Aristide's return to power.

Alerte, a young woman who was one of the thousands of victims thrown in a mass grave at Titanyen after her body was slashed with machetes, survived to see her president move up a few classes. She carries on her face and body the scarred symbols of repression and torture. She may wonder what went wrong, like most of us who fought and protested for the man we called a prophet of God. A man we believed in. A man we thought God sent to save us and Haiti.

Instead, his return satisfied his own ego, not the little people who have no one to turn to in Haiti. Why did he turn his back on the people? He built a center named after himself; the Aristide Center for Democracy sits next to his mansion while his supporters live in misery.

Why did Mr. Aristide, who came from peasant stock, marry Ms. Trouillot, who came from a well-known Haitian family of judges and lawyers?

Why? ◗

XI

Father,
you left behind
many swollen bellies.

Father,
you left behind
a country in turmoil.

Father,
you left with your hands
full of greenbacks.

Oh father!

RENDEZ-VOUS 2001

My mother still would not have cast her vote during the December 1995 presidential election, despite the presence of international troops and monitors. Old habits die hard. She lost hope in the so-called democratic system, especially after the coup d'état of September 1991. But many people opted to stay away from the polls because the flood — Lavalas — did not reach dry land as Aristide promised.

"Je prefere échouer avec le peuple au lieu de reussir sans lui," Aristide said. Translated, it meant he preferred peril with the people rather than succeed without them.

The coup destroyed Haiti, its economy and its people, but it was the best thing that happened to Aristide. The sad event gave him a chance to travel around the world, meet dignitaries, receive honorary degrees from colleges and universities in the name of democracy. It gave Aristide a golden opportunity to blame Haiti's tragedy on the coup. I wasn't surprised about the mismanagement that occurred during the 15 months of Aristide's administration, and the division in the Lavalas party.

At the end of Aristide's term, he started a campaign in Parliament to amend the constitution to allow him to make up the three years in office he lost while in exile. Preval, Aristide's former prime minister and a leading candidate for president, refused to support Aristide's bid to stay in power. Preval knew if Parliament passed a bill that would have allowed Aristide to stay in office to complete his term, he would have to wait three more years to run for president. This disagreement signaled the first signs of a strained relationship between the two friends. Aristide foolishly believed he would be allowed to remain in office. He pretended that his procrastination in organizing the presidential election was due to lack of funds.

Aristide, who spent 1,111 days in exile in Washington, thought he could outsmart his American caretakers by dragging his feet in planning elections. He failed to learn a basic lesson from his capitalist teachers — that a capitalist country makes exchanges, it doesn't give anything. He also forgot that the Clinton administration helped restore him to power on the condition that he would not violate the Haitian Constitution by seeking to stay in power for a second consecutive term. Clinton had pushed for Aristide's return, but not because of his love for him or Haitians in general. He needed a successful foreign policy mission to silence the critics who said he lacked foreign policy experience, especially after the debacle in Somalia.

Preval knew Aristide didn't want the election to take place. So Preval started to use Aristide's name to attract voters, because of Aristide's popularity among the poor. Aristide followers affectionately called him Titid, and Preval used this to his advantage. "Titid ak Preval se marasa" — Aristide and Preval are Twins — was the slogan that helped candidate Preval win the election.

Aristide reluctantly supported Preval, his friend and ally, shortly before the presidential election. Later, however, Aristide created his own political party, the Lavalas Family. Many believed the new party would give Aristide a head start in running for president in the year 2000. He was miffed that Preval began the process to sell the state companies, even though Aristide was the one who sold Haiti when he agreed to privatize businesses as a condition for his return to Haiti.

During his last 48 hours as president, Aristide looked like a candidate trying to capture undecided votes. He waited until his last day in office to unveil a statue dedicated to the victims of the September 1991 coup. The ceremony overshadowed president-elect Preval, his protégé, who had yet to be sworn into office as Aristide became a candidate for the year 2000. The majority of Aristide's supporters were from the poor neighborhoods. So the signs and banners that hung along the streets calling for Aristide to run for president again in five years must have been put up by invisible hands with money.

There were street signs that said: "Au revoir Titid a bientot," or "Bye Titid, see you soon." Also, "Titid nou fye de ou, rendevou 2001," which read as, "Titid, we are proud of you, we will meet in the year 2001."

It's unfortunate that once Haitian leaders taste power, they don't want to let go. As I see it, Aristide was no different than Raoul Cedras. I wonder why Haitian leaders refuse to unite and help Haiti get rid of its label as an international beggar?

As he attempted to hold on to power in the roughly 15 months left in his term, Aristide dragged his feet in making arrangements to sell the country's private companies as he promised while in exile. As a result, international aid was withheld, and Aristide's hands were tied in bringing economic growth to the impoverished island.

He accomplished little besides disbanding the military and replacing it with a national police force trained with the help of the U.S., which also had trained the former military. But the police force has no concept of human rights. They still kill and abuse innocent people. As I analyzed the situation, I concluded that the only role models the new, inexperienced police had were the brutal military police that terrorized the people for years. And they went free.

I hope Aristide gives to President Preval the 1,200 pages of documents compiled by the Commission of Truth and Justice, because Preval's government has to bring the perpetrators of violence to justice. Otherwise, the new, imported democracy Haitians live under will always be an illusion of peace.

While Aristide played his last political card, I decided to pay a visit to Chancerelles Gynecological and Obstetrics Center, where my four sisters, my brother and I were born. When I drove into the parking lot, I saw pigs and goats running around, and archaic ambulances parked in the driveway. I was surprised to see the hospital dilapidated. I asked my friend Leslie if the hospital was still open. Yes, he replied. I walked inside the facility and saw a group of pregnant women sitting on a long, wood bench in a dark corner waiting to see a doctor. A couple of doors down I saw a doctor doing paperwork behind a three-legged table covered with plastic.

"How are you, doc?" I asked.

"Fine," he said.

"I was born at this hospital," I said.

"That's great," he responded.

I asked him what had happened to the place that was once a wonderful hospital.

"Sir, I'm here so I can provide bread for my six kids," he said. "I'm not here to make any political statement."

His answer upset me and I told him so.

"Doc, how do you feel after spending years studying, you agree to work in this bird cage where mosquitoes make you dance?" I asked. "Don't you have any pride?"

He replied, this time in a soft voice, "Sir, I'm here to provide bread for my six kids. This is not my concern."

Without saying another word I moved toward the patient rooms where women slept in small spaces. I walked around and talked with them, although I knew I could do nothing for them. Everyone had economic problems but different physical ailments. The rooms were dark and hot with no indoor plumbing. On the way in I saw some women washing themselves outside with dirty water from an old bucket.

While talking to the women in the hospital, I heard a woman cry out, "Oh God, my Father, Oh God, my Father." I rushed to the next room to see what was going on. I couldn't believe what I saw. A woman with a man supporting her by the arm came toward me. She wore a white dress soaked in fresh blood. A pair of surgical scissors dangled from under her dress. I put my hand to my face and asked the man, who I later found out was her husband, what was wrong with her. He told me the woman had delivered twins but the doctor couldn't remove the placenta. The scissors were hanging from the placenta.

I asked if he could find a bed for her, but the man threw open his arms and said the doctor told him that walking would make the afterbirth come out. I told him the doctor was wrong and asked where I could find the doctor. On my way to the operating room in search of the doctor, I saw three women in labor accompanied by their mothers. They sat on the cement floor outside the operation room. I stopped for a moment and looked at them. I then entered the room and asked for the person in charge. A woman rudely asked what I wanted. I told her a woman was out there with scissors hanging from her private parts.

"Can you tell me what's going on?" I asked.

She said I was unauthorized to be in the hospital because I needed permission from the person in charge.

"Of course I got authorization from the minister," I said.

She said she was going to call his office but she called the police instead. He arrived with a long gun, took my hand and pushed me outside.

"What happened to democracy?" I screamed. "You are already killing it."

The police officer said if I didn't leave the hospital he would kill me like democracy.

Because I'm Haitian, I knew he could kill me just for fun and nothing would happen to him. I quickly left the hospital. This, after all, was Haiti.

I thought about all the events that had recently occurred in Haiti. It would take years before change would come to my country. I realized that the island I grew up in, the country I loved dearly, was a country in turmoil. ▶

XII

Does anyone care
that peasants use their sweat
to irrigate their plots of land?

Does anyone care
that simple diseases
are killing our people
like flies?

Does anyone care
that the population
is drowning in a cesspool
of illiteracy?

Does anyone care
for Haiti?

132

A COUNTRY IN TURMOIL

Haiti was in turmoil when my mother was born. It was still in turmoil after she died at the age of 72. And it will be in turmoil for a long time, even though President Rene Preval used the senseless propaganda during his inauguration at the National Palace. "Demokrasi simen, demokrasi pral donnen" — democracy sowed, democracy reaped. He made that statement to please his former boss, Jean-Bertrand Aristide, who had given him a snake without a head. Preval, an agronomist, should know that democracy is like a plant that needs roots to grow.

President Preval went out of his way to thank his predecessor for turning over to him a country in turmoil. Soon after he took office, renewed violence shook his government's ability to protect the vulnerable population. The atmosphere was reminiscent of the days when anarchy prevailed in the aftermath of the coup.

Unlike his predecessor, Preval didn't have the backing of the masses, although he came from the same political party as Aristide, Organization Political Lavalas, which grew out of the Lavalas movement.

In early 1998, the national police couldn't control violent outbursts that left civilians and police officers dead. It left me asking many questions: What are the international troops doing in the country? Why can't they try to put a stop to all the crime that's taking place in Haiti now? Perhaps they want to collect more checks. What will happen when all the United Nations' mission leaves the country? There have been threats that armed opposition groups will bring more violence. Will the inexperienced, corrupt and poorly trained national police be able to control the expected violence?

The country is again on the verge of civil unrest. There are no jobs. People are afraid for their lives. Inflation is raging. Most of the public school teachers haven't received their monthly salaries for nearly a year. In the meantime, Preval, his staff and members of Parliament continue to get their monthly checks.

Is this democracy?

Politicians don't care that the majority can't read and write. It is easier to manipulate and oppress an ignorant people. How can a country with a population that's 85 percent illiterate, with an unemployment rate of 80 percent, progress?

The 13 candidates who opposed Preval watch as the country dies day by day. They're waiting for the opportunity to run for president again in 2000. Preval tried very hard to show that he's a man of the people. But you can't be the man while you let people die of hunger. "Sak vid pa kanpé." It means, "Empty bags can't stand." It is a popular saying in Haiti. Even Preval doesn't feel secure; he has about 30 bodyguards who accompany him everywhere he goes.

In July 1996, I, Franki and a friend of ours were on our way to the countryside one day when we saw a crowd of people. We parked the rented sports utility vehicle on the side of the road and got out. Someone told us Preval was touring a poor neighborhood to see what needed to be done. I began to take pictures of the president and his entourage. The bodyguards told me to stop. I told them I was only doing my job. I continued to pursue Preval until one of the bodyguards pointed an automatic

rifle to my belly. He told me if I clicked the camera one more time, he would shoot me. I returned to the truck visibly shaken, and murmured something about the lack of democracy.

Franki was upset with me because she had pleaded with me to stop before I got killed. No picture, she said, is worth dying for. We knew then that things hadn't changed in Haiti.

The country faces horrifying troubles. Its ministries are inept. Its Parliament is paralyzed by corruption and inexperience. Its greedy leaders are taking advantage of the problems that divide Preval's administration, mainly uncontrolled violence and disagreement over privatization of national companies. Its national police resembles the military thugs it replaced. Its justice system is tainted by crooked judges. Its people are dying of starvation. Its perverse elite grows wealthier and wealthier from profligate monopolies. Its leadership is virtually nonexistent.

This is a shadowgraph of Haiti, a country whose people have been shackled during an almost 200-year struggle for democracy. During the Duvalier era, the Tonton Macoutes beat to death members of grass-roots organizations. Today, the Lavalas movement, the so-called party of the poor, has dissociated itself from the masses.

We have a democratic government and people are still dying of hunger and thirsting for freedom. The flood of the Lavalas movement that burst forth on Dec. 16, 1990, is dry. What a shame for the party of the people.

Wé pa wé fok peyi a vanse. ❿

PHOTOGRAPHY INDEX

COVER

Eyewitness

Two brothers look through a large crack in an old mill at L'Artibonite, about 100 miles north of Port-au-Prince, Haiti. Fear remained in the eyes of the brothers, who saw members of FRAPH kill and terrorize the community shortly after President Jean-Bertrand Aristide arrived.

PREFACE

In Memory of My Brother

Andre Colin holds two lighted candles in memory of his brother, who was killed by paramilitary thugs.

Agent of Death

A FRAPH member holds a machine gun during an anti-Aristide protest in front of the National Palace. The FRAPH members became agents of death during the military reign.

Dancing Coffin

A group of men hired by a funeral director carry a coffin to a family's home in preparation for a wake the day before the funeral. The men dance in the streets with the coffin. Death has become a part of life in Haiti.

CHAPTER-1

In My Mother's Footsteps

Saprina Joseph, 15, makes a living carrying baskets of goods in Gonaives, Haiti, like her mother did.

Headstrong

A peasant carries goods while walking the streets of Port-au-Prince. She goes house to house selling goods.

Backbreaking

A woman pushes her produce in a wheelbarrow to the market in L'Archaie, Haiti.

Corn Mill

A peasant grinds corn at a mill. She will sell the corn at the street market in L'Artibonite.

Mother Of Democracy

Haiti's first woman president, Ertha Pascal-Trouillot. (Photo courtesy Pascal-Trouillot.)

CHAPTER-2

Vote

A little girl washes her clothes under a sign that simply reads "Vote."

Running Campaign

A group of people run in the street with campaign signs during an election day in Port-au-Prince.

CHAPTER-3

Sitting Tall

A group of Aristide's bodyguards carry him on their shoulders after he voted in the Dec. 16, 1995, presidential election.

The Worshipers

Odette Examour, left, and Christiane Charles, right, pray at St. Gerard Catholic Church one day after President Aristide returned to Haiti. This was the first time in three years that worshipers were allowed to celebrate, without violence, the anniversary of the parish which advocated the theology of liberation.

CHAPTER-4

Mon General

Lt. Gen. Raoul Cedras and his wife, Yanick, stand in front of Notre Dame Cathedral during the Batailles de Vertieres and Armed Forces Day celebrations.

Shoeshine Kit

Haitian soldiers keep Alix Jean busy with his shoeshine kit.

Symbol of Repression

The abolished Haitian military tank, a symbol of repression, shown during a parade.

The Last Parade

The defunct Haitian military participates in its last parade.

The Wake

A woman views the body of a young Haitian boy who drowned in the ocean while attempting to come to America with his family. The wake was held on 54th Street in Miami's Little Haiti.

CHAPTER-5

Kneeling for Democracy

A Haitian demonstrator pleads for democracy during a protest in front of the White House. He was among thousands of Haitians who traveled to Washington to support then-exiled President Aristide.

President to President

Exiled Haitian President Jean-Bertrand Aristide negotiates his return to power with President Bill Clinton at the White House.

The Price of Democracy

A woman nurses her husband at General Hospital. He was wounded by a paramilitary member during the fight for democracy.

Shadow Of Misery

Mirlande Sanon, 10, holds her little brother, Jean, 2, at Archaie, Haiti while their mother, Levoicia Joseph, waits for a miracle to feed them. Joseph has five children.

God Is Watching You

The Rev. Gerard Jean Juste, ex-director of Miami's Haitian Refugee Center, leads a protest in the city's Little Haiti.

Hard Labor

Two women are supported by their mother at Issaie Jeanty Hospital, which has few beds. Most patients sleep on benches until they give birth, and some babies are born on the hospital's cement floor.

Difficult Birth

A woman who gave birth the night before walks in Issaie Jeanty Hospital with her umbilical cord hanging, while her husband carries the IV bag. Her husband said the doctor told her to walk around the hospital so the cord would fall out.

No Aristide, No Peace

An Aristide supporter sports a "No Aristide, No Peace" button.

Mister Clean

De facto Prime Minister Marc Bazin, "Mister Clean," and his wife Mirlande leave Notre Dame Cathedral during Batailles de Vertieres and Armed Forces Day celebrations.

Chapter-6

Partners in Slavery
Onelus Ridore and his old friend, Jean Novembre, left Haiti together in the 1950s to work in the Dominican Republic sugar cane fields. They never returned home.

My Machete
Eric St. Vil holds his machete in a sugar cane field where he works.

Working for Nothing
Francisco Francois works in a sugar cane field for almost nothing at the Palma Rajo batey in the Dominican Republic.

Lifelessness at the Batey
A typical lifeless day for the St. Vil family, who live in a batey.

Makeshift Stove
Ramonita Nelson cooks on a makeshift stove outside a row house in a batey.

Slave Quarters
Haitian sugar-cane cutters stand outside a slave quarter at Las Pajas Batey in the Dominican Republic.

Chapter-7

Peace-Breaker
An American military police officer who is part of the peacekeeping force fights with a young Haitian in front of the Industrial Park in Port-au-Prince.

Home Alone
A homeless boy sleeps in front of the National Palace. He is one of thousands of tiny heroes who eat and sleep anywhere.

Under Control
U.S. Marines take control of Port-au-Prince streets

Hopehold
A mural describes the U.S. invasion of Haiti in 1994.

Chapter-8

Begging for Forgiveness
A mural of ex-Lt. Gen. Raoul Cedras begging Aristide for forgiveness, while former Brig. Gen. Philippe Biamby and former Police Chief Michel Francois stand in the background.

Toy Soldiers
Three boys mimic the Haitian military in front of the Fort Dimanche barracks in Port-au-Prince.

Adieu, Generals
Generals Raoul Cedras and Philippe Biamby salute the flag while the military band plays the Haitian national anthem in front of military headquarters. They left Haiti for Panama on a jet chartered by the U.S. military.

Chapter-9

What My Father Died For?
A woman cries for her father during a memorial service at Sacre Heart Catholic Church in Port-au-Prince. Her father was killed along with Minister of Justice Guy Malary by a paramilitary group.

Under the U.S. Guns
President Jean-Bertrand Aristide, returning from exile under the U.S. guns, waves to the crowd after a brief ceremony at Port-au-Prince International Airport. He boarded a U.S. helicopter that took him to the presidential palace.

Our Misery is Over
Haitians sing "Our misery is over, Titid returns" in front of the National Palace on Oct. 15, 1994.

Democracy or Demagogy
A woman holds upside down a sign that promotes democracy in front of the National Palace while President Aristide makes a speech about reconciliation.

CHAPTER-10

The President's Guest
Aristide puts his arm around Elira, a bread vendor he invited into his mansion in Tabarre. He met her after he voted during the presidential elections in 1995.

Homework
Big sister helps little sister with her homework on the trunk of an old car because there is no electricity in their house.

Laborer
A little boy uses his hands to work the land before he plants rice at L'Artibonite. He works 12 hours a day for 15 gourdes.

Royal Couple
Jean-Bertrand Aristide and his wife, Mildred, during his last day as president of Haiti.

CHAPTER-11

Farewell
Aristide waves goodbye from a U.N. helicopter after Rene Preval's inauguration on Feb. 7, 1996.

Fenced Out
Two little girls peer through a fence surrounding the National Palace as Aristide bids farewell.

An Open Eye
Aristide and Preval share a moment together during the transition of presidential power at the National Palace.

CHAPTER-12

Helping Hands
Majorie, 13, helps her mother make cassava at Carrefour, Haiti. The girl doesn't attend school because her mother cannot afford to send her.

Pass It On
Rene Preval hugs Aristide after Preval was sworn in as president at the Legislative Palace.

Bread on Wheels
Viton Cadet carries a basket of bread on his head while riding his bicycle on a road in Leogane, Haiti. He rides more than 20 miles a day selling bread door to door.

Gun and Gun
A woman waves a gun while protesting against Aristide's government.

I Promise . . .
Rene Preval leaves the Legislative Palace after being sworn in as president of Haiti. He promised to restore respect in the government.

Wé Pa Wé
On their way to school, two young girls pass a mural at the military barracks in Port-au-Prince.